W9-BOB-026

Voluntary Carbon Markets

The Ecosystem Marketplace seeks to become the world's leading source of information on markets and payment schemes for ecosystem services (services such as water quality, carbon sequestration and biodiversity). We believe that by providing reliable information on prices, regulation, science, and other market-relevant factors, markets for ecosystem services will one day become a fundamental part of our economic system, helping give value to environmental services that, for too long, have been taken for granted. In providing useful market information, we hope not only to facilitate transactions, but also to catalyze new thinking, spur the development of new markets, and achieve effective and equitable nature conservation. The Ecosystem Marketplace is a project of Forest Trends.

www.ecosystemmarketplace.com

Voluntary Carbon Markets
An International Business Guide to What They Are and How They Work

Written and edited by
Ricardo Bayon, Amanda Hawn
and
Katherine Hamilton

London • Sterling, VA

First published by Earthscan in the UK and USA in 2007

ISBN: 1-84407-417-X hardback
978-1-84407-417-0 hardback

Typesetting by 4word Ltd, Bristol
Printed and bound in the UK by TJ International Ltd, Padstow, Cornwall
Cover design by Andrew Corbett

For a full list of publications please contact:

Earthscan
8–12 Camden High Street
London, NW1 0JH, UK
Tel: +44 (0)20 7387 8558
Fax: +44 (0)20 7387 8998
Email: earthinfo@earthscan.co.uk
Web: www.earthscan.co.uk

22883 Quicksilver Drive, Sterling, VA 20166-2012, USA

Earthscan is an imprint of James and James (Science Publishers) Ltd and publishes in association with the International Institute for Environment and Development

A catalogue record for this book is available from the British Library

Library of Congress Cataloging-in-Publication Data
Voluntary carbon markets : an international business guide to what they are and how they work / edited by Ricardo Bayon, Amanda Hawn and Katherine Hamilton.
p. cm
Covers the U.S., Europe, Australia, Canada, and Asia, what the markets are, how they work, and their business potential to help slow climate change.
Includes index.
ISBN-13: 978-1-84407-417-4 (hardback)
ISBN-10: 1-84407-417-X (hardback)
1. Emissions trading. 2. Environmental impact charges. 3. Carbon dioxide mitigation–Economic aspects. 4. Greenhouse gases–Economic aspects. 5. Climatic changes–Economic aspects. I. Bayon, Ricardo. II. Hawn, Amanda. III. Hamilton, Katherine.
HC79.P55V65 2006
363.738′746–dc22 2006029027

This publication is printed on FSC certified paper.
FSC (The Forest Stewardship Council) is an international network to promote responsible management of the world's forests.

The Ecosystem Marketplace will offset greenhouse gas emissions directly resulting from the publication of this book.

Printed on totally chlorine-free paper

Contents

List of Figures, Tables and Boxes

Figures

Tables

Boxes

List of Contributors

Dr David Brand is the founder and Managing Director of New Forests, a forestry asset management and advisory business based in Sydney, Australia (see www.newforests.com.au). The firm represents institutional and private equity investors in forestry and land management, specializing in investment programmes that can link to environmental markets related to carbon, water and biodiversity. New Forests also operates an advisory business that supports environmental market policies, business plans and transactions, advising both buyers and sellers of carbon offsets.

Martha Isabel Ruiz Corzo, a former music teacher, founded the Grupo Ecologico Sierra Gorda in 1989 along with her husband and a group of neighbours. The first director of the Grupo Ecologico, she led the effort to obtain the decree of the Sierra Gorda as a Biosphere Reserve, obtained in 1997. As a result of this, she was named by the President of Mexico as the first director of the Sierra Gorda Biosphere Reserve. A recognized social entrepreneur, Ruiz is an outspoken advocate for the development of payments for environmental services programmes that work in areas of extreme poverty. She is a member of the board of directors of Forest Trends.

Robert Harmon serves as Vice President of Renewable Energy Programs for the Bonneville Environmental Foundation (BEF), where he is credited with developing BEF's Green Tag program, which began in 1999. In 2001, Robert designed and launched BEF's CO_2 calculator, the first such calculator on the internet. In 2004, Robert was awarded the national Green Power Pioneer Award for his efforts to build a thriving and credible Green Tag market in the US. Robert has worked in the fields of energy productivity and renewables since 1987. He has served as the Chairman of the American Wind Energy Association's Small Wind Turbine Committee, and as a member of the California Emerging Renewables Advisory Board. He currently serves on the Board of the Northwest Energy Coalition and on the Advisory Board for the Environment & Alternative Energy Cluster Working Group of the Puget Sound Regional Council.

Ben Henneke is President of Clean Air Action Corporation (CAAC), a company that has created NO_x, VOC, PM and CO_2 reductions. CAAC, along with the Institute for Environmental Innovation, funds the TIST

Programme, which is creating superior CO_2 offsets with biodiversity, desertification and economic development benefits. See www.tist.org.

Erin Meezan is the manager of environmental affairs for Interface. In this capacity she provides technical assistance and policy support to Interface's global business units on a range of sustainability issues. She manages Interface's external partnerships with environmental stakeholders on climate change and renewable energy issues, and advises Interface's internal Sustainability Council as chair of its renewable energy front. She manages Interface's corporate GHG Inventory and their carbon offset portfolio to meet corporate and product climate neutral goals. She has a Masters in Environmental Policy and a Juris Doctor from Vermont Law School.

Marisa Meizlish is the Manager of Advisory Services at New Forests and has a BA in journalism and political science from Northwestern University in Chicago, and a Masters in Environmental Management from the University of New South Wales. Marisa previously worked in the news media and public relations fields in New York and Chicago.

Dr Janet Peace is a senior research fellow in the eEconomics Program at the Pew Center on Global Climate Change. At Pew she serves as the in-house economist and together with the Director of Policy Analysis coordinates the Center's research on the economic modelling of climate change policies. As part of this role, she provides quantitative analysis of policy proposals, assessing relative merits and dissecting underlying assumptions. She is also responsible for communicating these results to policy makers, academic researchers and business leaders, by means of reports, briefings and presentations. Prior to coming to the Pew Center, Dr Peace was the Director of Offsets Development and Industry Relations with a Canadian non-profit group, Climate Change Central. Here she worked on issues related to implementation of the Kyoto Protocol, including the assessment of cost effective, alternative policies that were politically feasible for industry and all levels of government. Working with these stakeholders, she was a founding Chair of the National Offsets Quantification Team – an intergovernmental/industry group currently developing standardized offset quantification protocols for use in the Canadian offset system.

Dr Alexander Rau is a founding partner of Climate Wedge Ltd Oy. Climate Wedge Ltd is a scientific adviser to the Cheyne Carbon Fund. The Cheyne Carbon Fund is a voluntary carbon fund, managed by Cheyne Capital Management Limited, which contains a diversified global portfolio of high quality emissions reductions for use as carbon offsets by corporate and institutional buyers. Alexander was previously part of the Climate Change Services team in PricewaterhouseCoopers's Energy Corporate Finance practice in London, and subsequently formed an independent consulting group in 2003 with other senior members to advise clients such as McKinsey & Company and CSIRO on carbon-related issues. Alexander has a PhD in physics from Oxford University, where he studied on a Marshall Scholarship and NSF graduate research fellowship, and a BA from Cornell University.

David Ross, originally from the state of Ohio in the United States, has worked for non-profit organizations for more than 18 years, including the American Civil Liberties Union of San Diego & Imperial Counties, the American Cancer Society, Butte Environmental Council, Parks & Preserves Foundation and National Wildlife Federation. He has been working on the project of biodiversity conservation in the Sierra Gorda Biosphere Reserve since 2003. He led negotiations on behalf of Bosque Sustentable for its sale of emission reduction credits to the United Nations Foundation.

Jonathan Shopley is CEO of The CarbonNeutral Company. Prior to joining The CarbonNeutral Company in 2001, he held the position of Managing Director and Vice President in the European division of Arthur D. Little, the technology and management consulting company. Before entering management, Jonathan was an environmental engineer focused on the development of technologies for the mitigation of environmental impacts in industry.

Lorna Slade is with Group Corporate Affairs, HSBC Holdings plc. HSBC Holdings is developing a sustainability-focused business in a number of areas, particularly low carbon energy, water infrastructure, sustainable forestry and related agricultural commodities. It has also recently announced a strategy to help its clients respond to the challenges and opportunities of creating a lower carbon economy – advising them on the implications of climate change and the business opportunities that arise. In 2005, HSBC was the first bank to become carbon neutral.

Dr Mark Trexler has more than 25 years of energy and environmental experience, and has focused on global climate change since joining the World Resources Institute in 1988. He is now President of Trexler Climate + Energy Services, which provides strategic, market and project services to clients around the world.

Ben Vitale is an experienced finance, operations and technology Executive. He holds an MBA from Northwestern University's Kellogg School of Management and a BSc in computer and electrical engineering from Purdue University. Within Conservation International's Center for Environmental Leadership in Business, Ben is driving change to create new financial instruments for corporations, market makers and financing institutions to fully value and fund the ecological services provided by intact and restored ecosystems. In particular, Mr Vitale is working to develop investment grade Conservation Carbon projects in Madagascar, Ecuador, China, Brazil and other biodiversity hotspots.

Walker Wright is founder of Amelio Solutions, an advisory group focusing on international photovoltaic project development and financing. Walker has also served as business development and marketing consultant to Terra Solar North America and Renewable Energy Solutions, Inc. (RESI), two industry leaders in thin-film photovoltaic manufacturing and research. Walker holds a BA from Princeton University and an MSc from The London School of Economics. Walker lives in San Francisco and does not own a car.

Acknowledgements

Ricardo Bayon

Like most books, this one is years in the making and has many parents. It was first born, however, of the realization that, while there was much talk of the regulated carbon markets, the voluntary markets were being left behind. This, despite the fact that these markets appeared to be growing rapidly. But knowing that something needed to be done and getting it done were two very far-removed destinations. Getting the book to this stage would simply not have been possible without the unflagging support of Michael Jenkins and the rest of our colleagues at Forest Trends. Likewise, none of this would have happened were it not for the generous contributions of many donors to the Ecosystem Marketplace. These include:

ABN-AMRO
Conservation International
The Citigroup Foundation
O Boticario
The David and Lucile Packard Foundation
The Gordon and Betty Moore Foundation
The Nature Conservancy
The UK Department for International Development
The UK Forestry Commission
The US Forest Service; and
The US Natural Resources Conservation Service (NRCS)

Our deepest thanks to all of them for being more than sponsors; for being true partners.

Also, it should be mentioned that a tremendous amount of work that went into this book came from a report prepared for the Ecosystem Marketplace by David Brand and Marisa Meizlich at New Forests. Without that initial impetus, this book wouldn't have been possible. Likewise, I would like to thank, in no particular order, Jason Scott, Colin Le Duc, David Tepper, Richard Burrett, Mark Trexler, Mark Kenber, Renat Heuberger, Richard Tipper, Jessica Orrego, Toby Janson-Smith, Jonathan Shopley, Bill Sneyd, Alex Rau, Michael Schlup, and all of the contributors to this book for their openness and willingness to share both intelligence and information. Their excitement for these markets is contagious.

As anyone who knows them (and me) will tell you, this book would not be half as good as it is if it weren't for my co-authors, Amanda Hawn and Katherine Hamilton. Their writing skills and insights make this book what it is.

Last, but never least, I'd like to thank my wife Nathalie and son Luka for their support and forbearance. This book has meant many hours travelling and writing; hours away from them. Without a doubt, for me, this has been the most painful and costly part of the book's production process. May my time away from them in the future be brief.

Amanda Hawn

Many people helped with the creation of this book, but Peter Barnes and the managers of The Mesa Refuge – who provided the space to sit down and finally write – top the list of those to whom gratitude is due. All of the contributors to the fourth chapter of the book were generous with their time, energy and insight – for all of these things, the authors are thankful. In addition to those whose names appear as guest contributors, we are grateful to the many others who took the time to return phone calls, give interviews, provide statistics and generally enrich the information herein. We are grateful, too, to Marion Yuen who organized a great conference – the Green T Forum – about many of the topics covered in this book in May of 2006. Walker Wright and Nathan Larsen stayed up to burn the midnight oil during the final editing phases of the manuscript, and Rob West and his team at Earthscan were both patient and professional – thank you. Last but not least, I would like to extend my gratitude to my co-editors – Ricardo Bayon and Katherine Hamilton - who are as kind and professional, as they are intelligent.

Katherine Hamilton

My gratitude goes to Ricardo Bayon and Amanda Hawn, two talented and innovative individuals, for the opportunity to contribute to this exciting project and the work of Ecosystem Marketplace. I'd also like express my sincere appreciation to Brad Gentry and many others at the Yale School of Forestry and Environmental Studies, who fostered my research on carbon markets. Many thanks also go to the numerous experts in this market, including Lars Kvale, Mark Trexler, Toby Jason-Smith, John Kunz and Erin Meezan, who willingly took the time to educate, patiently answer questions and offer insights into this evolving marketplace.

Foreword

The serious debate over the climate crisis has now moved on from the question of whether it exists to how we can craft emergency solutions in order to avoid catastrophic damage.

The debate over solutions has been slow to start in earnest because some of our leaders still find it more convenient to deny the reality of the crisis. The hard truth for the rest of us is that the maximum that seems politically feasible still falls far short of the minimum that would be effective in solving the crisis.

T. S. Eliot once wrote:

> *Between the idea and the reality, Between the motion and the act Falls the Shadow. Between the conception and the creation, Between the emotion and the response Falls the Shadow.*

Leaders must try to shine some light on a pathway through this terra incognita that lies between where we are and where we need to go.

Outside of the Kyoto Treaty, business leaders in both political parties have taken significant steps to position their companies as leaders in addressing this crisis and have adopted policies that not only reduce CO_2 but make their companies zero carbon. Many of them have discovered a way to increase profits and productivity by eliminating their contributions to global warming pollution. A key contributor to the movement to freeze and then reduce carbon emissions and a remarkable area of commercial and policy innovation, is the voluntary carbon market.

Voluntary Carbon Markets by Ricardo Bayon, Amanda Hawn and Katherine Hamilton describes a remarkable area of innovation in the fight to control global warming pollution in describing the foundations upon which many promising carbon reducing strategies have been built. And in the current absence of a worldwide regulatory system for carbon reduction, *Voluntary Carbon Markets* also foreshadows the factors which will drive the next generation of market-based innovation for fighting global warming pollution. I commend the work of Ricardo and the Ecosystem Marketplace Group for jumping into T. S. Eliot's void and shining the light on this important market.

The climate crisis is not a political issue. It is a moral issue. It affects the survival of human civilization. It is not a question of left versus right; it is a question of right versus wrong. Put simply, it is wrong to destroy the habitability of our planet and ruin the prospects of every generation that follows ours.

What is motivating millions of global citizens to think differently about solutions to the climate crisis is the growing realization that this challenge is bringing us unprecedented opportunity.

This is an opportunity for transcendence, an opportunity to find our better selves and in rising to meet this challenge, create a better brighter future – a future worthy of the generations who come after us and who have a right to be able to depend on us.

Al Gore

List of Acronyms and Abbreviations

BEF	Bonneville Environmental Foundation
CBD	Convention on Biological Diversity
CCAR	California Climate Action Registry
CCB	Climate, Community and Biodiversity Alliance
CCX	Chicago Climate Exchange
CDM	Clean Development Mechanism
CDP	Carbon Disclosure Project
CEI	Community Energy Inc.
CER	Certified Emissions Reductions
CERES	Coalition for Environmentally Responsible Economies
CFI	Carbon Financial Instruments
CO_2	carbon dioxide
COP	Conference of the Parties
CRS	Center for Resource Solutions
ERT	Environmental Resources Trust
ERUs	Emission Reduction Units
EU ETS	European Union Emission Trading Scheme
EUA	European Union Allowances
GHG	greenhouse gas
GPS	Global Positioning System
GSV	Gold Standard for Voluntary Emission Reductions (GSV)
GWh	gigawatt hours
GWP	global warming potential
IETA	International Emissions Trading Association
JI	Joint Implementation
kWh	kilowatt hour
MDGs	Millennium Development Goals
Mt	million tons
MWh	megawatt hour
NGO	non-governmental organization
NO_x	Nitrogen oxides
NPA	Natural Protected Area (in Mexico)
NREL	National Renewable Energy Laboratory
NSW	New South Wales

PDA	Personal Digital Assistant
ppm	parts per million
REC	Renewable Energy Certificate
RECs	Renewable Energy Certificates
REN21	Renewable Energy Policy Network for the 21st Century
RGGI	Regional Greenhouse Gas Initiative
ROCs	Renewable Obligation Certificates
RPS	Renewable Portfolio Standards
SO_2	sulfur dioxide
SRI	Socially Responsible Investment
tCO_2e	metric tons of carbon dioxide equivalent
TIST	International Small Group and Tree Planting Alliance
UNEP	United Nations Environment Programme
VCS	Voluntary Carbon Standard
VER	Verified Emissions Reduction
WBCSD	World Business Council for Sustainable Development
WRI	World Resources Institute

Introduction

After decades of searching for creative and innovative ways to protect the environment, it is time we be brutally honest with ourselves: We are losing this battle, and losing it in a spectacular way. Every day we hear that yet another species has gone extinct, yet another acre of forest has disappeared, and yet another coral reef has been destroyed. And as if that weren't enough, Earth has begun warming to such an extent that climate, sea levels, glacial ice, and even the polar ice caps may be in danger. It is enough to demoralize even the most determined optimist.

But this is a battle we cannot afford to lose – literally. It is time not to give up, but to redouble our efforts, to become more creative, and to seek new ways of working together in situations where confrontation is no longer effective (if it ever was). The time, in other words, has come for the environmental equivalent of the St Crispin's day speech in Shakespeare's Henry V, a call to arms that does not lament how difficult the task is likely to be – or how few of us there are – but rather pushes us forward into the wild and scary unknown.

And, in the case of the environmental movement, the scary unknown is the use of markets and market-like instruments to protect the environment. To be fair, we now have nearly two decades of experimentation in the use of market mechanisms for environmental protection. The US Acid Rain trading scheme began in the 1980s, and various forms of market-like mechanisms for environmental protection have been tried all over the world.

But the game is one of scale. Protecting one species, one piece of land, one watershed may be important, but it is no longer enough. The solutions today need to be systemic, they need to change the way we do business, the way we eat, drink, sleep, and think. And this is where we think markets may hold the greatest promise.

Some years ago, we created Forest Trends with a vision. Our vision was simple: we believed that by bringing loggers, environmentalists, businesspeople, academics, and scientists together into the same room to think about issues that mattered to all of them we would be better able to stem the loss of the world's forests. But we soon realized that – effective as this might be – it was not enough. We saw that in order to save the world's forests, society needed to value standing forests as least as highly as it values soybeans, cattle ranches, logging operations, and the other alternatives driving deforestation. As the saying goes, in the end, we will only protect what we value.

Initially, some of our friends in the environmental movement accused us of heresy. How could we want to put a value on nature? Nature, they felt, is and should always be priceless. And while we agree with the sentiment, in practice, our economic system doesn't see nature as priceless, it assigns it a value, a value that is awfully close to zero. In short, our society (or at least our economic system) is confusing priceless with worthless.

Having come to the realization that we needed to 'internalize the economic value' (to use the academic jargon) of nature, we quickly saw that one of the most effective ways to achieve this was through the use of markets or market-like instruments.

And so in 2000 we brought together a small group of people from around the world in the beautiful mountains of New South Wales, Australia, in a town called Katoomba, to discuss the role markets and payments for ecosystem services had to play in forest conservation. True to our roots, we made sure this group included people from all walks of life: bankers, businesspeople, government officials, academics, community leaders, non-profits ... the entire spectrum. And from this meeting was born the Katoomba Group. At that time few people were talking about markets and payments for ecosystem services. Remember, this was five years before the European Union's Emissions Trading Scheme was but a glint in anyone's eye. Even Kyoto, at the time, looked set to flounder.

In this way, the Katoomba Group became a stimulating place to refine our vision, define our strategies, and so we continued to meet once or twice a year in either a large market for forest goods and services (London, Tokyo, Switzerland), or a large producer of these services (Brazil, Vancouver, Thailand). As time went by the group grew and our understanding of our subject deepened. We realized that what we were talking about went much further than forests, that it was a systemic problem affecting all ecosystems, and we realized that in order to thrive, environmental markets need science, finance, expertise, and, most especially, information. That is why we created the Ecosystem Marketplace, a tool that we hope will become a kind of 'Bloomberg' for the world's environmental markets.

All of this is a long-winded attempt to give you a bit of the background for the book you now hold in your hands. It was born of environmental need and it seeks to further deepen our understanding of one portion of the carbon markets that we think has been grossly overlooked: the voluntary carbon market.

But it is part of something bigger, part of our attempts to come up with (and better understand) a series of tools – environmental markets and market-like mechanisms – that may help us succeed where other tools have so far failed to conserve the ecosystems on which we all depend. So, once more into the breach, but this time, let's arm ourselves in the most effective way possible. Let's use markets – both voluntary and regulated – and payments for ecosystem services where they make sense to help us address climate change and other seemingly insurmountable problems. Because – like King Henry said at

Agincourt – one day, we will look back and either be happy we did, or else wish we had; the choice is ours.

Michael Jenkins
President,
Forest Trends

Ricardo Bayon
Managing Director
Ecosystem Marketplace

1

The Big Picture

For hurricane watchers, 2005 was a year for the record books. A startling number of hurricanes hit the Gulf of Mexico, causing over US$100 billion in damages. Hurricane Katrina alone displaced 1 million people and left 1,000 dead.

The 2004 hurricane season was a bit less horrific in terms of raw numbers, but what it lacked in quantity, it made up for in oddity; the year was marked by an event some believed to be a scientific impossibility, namely a hurricane in the southern Atlantic. For over 40 years, weather satellites circling the globe have seen hurricanes and cyclones in the north Atlantic, and on both sides of the equator in the Pacific, but never – until 2004 – in the southern Atlantic. On 28 March, Hurricane Catarina slammed into Brazil, proving that recent weather patterns are starkly different from those of the 20th century.

What is going on? Are these freak occurrences or signs of something bigger?

While there is no level of data or anecdote that that will satisfy hardened sceptics, many scientists now believe that the storms of 2004 and 2005 are merely symptoms of a bigger problem: global climate change. As the Earth's average temperature grows warmer, they say, atmospheric and oceanic patterns are beginning to shift, fueling increased storms and unusual weather events.

Temperatures at the planet's surface increased by an estimated 1.4 degrees Fahrenheit (°F) (0.8 degrees Celsius (°C)) between 1900 and 2005. The past decade was the hottest on record during the last 150 years, and 2005 was the hottest year of the last 150 years (Linden, 2006).

Again, sceptics argue that this is part of the natural variability in the Earth's temperature, but the majority of scientists now agree that it is more likely due to increased concentrations of heat-trapping greenhouse gases (GHGs) in the atmosphere.

Box 1.1 A Look at the Science

Prior to the industrial revolution of the 18th and 19th centuries, the atmospheric concentration of carbon dioxide (CO_2) was approximately 280 parts per million (ppm). Today, the atmospheric concentration of CO_2 has risen to 380ppm, largely because of anthropogenic emissions from the burning of fossil fuels used in transportation, agriculture, energy generation and the production of everyday materials. The loss of natural carbon sinks (places where carbon is pulled out of the atmosphere and trapped either in geological formations or in biological organisms) – on land and in the ocean – is also contributing to increased levels of carbon dioxide in the atmosphere.

The rapid rise in concentration of CO_2 in the atmosphere concerns scientists because CO_2 is a greenhouse gas. GHGs allow sunlight to enter the atmosphere, but they keep the heat released from the Earth's surface from getting back out.

While recent trends show a gradual warming trend of the Earth's surface, some scientists fear future climate change will not be linear. 'The Earth's system', says Wallace Broecker, Newberry Professor of Earth and Environmental Sciences at Columbia University, 'has sort of proven that if it's given small nudges, it can take large leaps. By tripling the amount of carbon dioxide in the atmosphere, we are giving the system a huge nudge.' (Hawn, 2004).

The 'large leaps' to which Broecker refers are better known as 'abrupt climate changes' in the world of science. Over the course of thousands of years, such changes have left geological records of themselves in ice cores and stalagmites. These records show that past temperature swings on our planet have been as large as 18°F (–7.8°C) and have occurred over time scales as short as two years.

Using the analogy of a car moving along an unknown road at night, Klaus Lackner, a geophysicist at Columbia University, argues that our incomplete understanding of the natural system is no excuse for delaying action: 'We sort of vaguely see in the headlights a sharp turn. There are two possibilities.

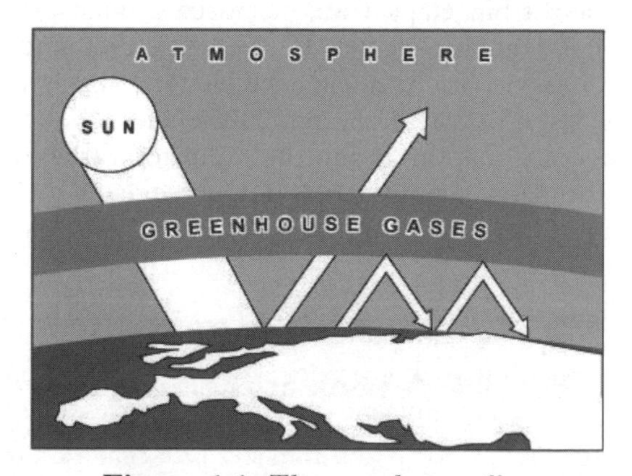

Figure 1.1 *The greenhouse effect*

Source: Pew Center on Global Climate Change (2001) 'The greenhouse effect', In Claussen, E. (ed) *Climate Change: Science, Strategies and Solutions*, Brill, Boston

You can say: 'I'm going to ignore that and keep going at 90 miles an hour because you cannot prove to me that the curve is not banked and therefore I might make it . . . or you can put on the brakes.' (Hawn, 2004).

Noting that there could be an oil slick and no bank to the road, Lackner says the good news is that we have the technology to put on the brakes. He adds, however, that if we want to stabilize the amount of CO_2 in the atmosphere at double the natural level (roughly 500ppm, which still might leave us with an ice-free Arctic Ocean), we have to start now (Hawn, 2004).

Market theory

To start towards stabilized levels of atmospheric CO_2, policy makers argue that we not only need to prime the research pump behind clean energy technologies and emission reduction strategies, we also must generate the market pull for them.

Enter the global carbon market. Many think markets for emissions reductions are among the most innovative and cost-effective means society has of creating a market pull for new clean energy technologies while, at the same time, putting a price on pollution and thereby providing incentives for people to emit less.

The theory is that carbon markets are able to achieve this magic because they help channel resources toward the most cost effective means of reducing GHG emissions. At the same time, they punish (monetarily) those who emit more than an established quota, and reward (again, monetarily) those who emit less. In so doing, they encourage people to emit less and change the economics of energy technologies, making technologies that emit less carbon more competitive vis-à-vis their carbon-intensive counterparts.

There is other magic at work as well: By turning units of pollution into units of property, the system makes it possible to exchange pollution from Cape Town with pollution from Cape Cod. If business managers find reducing their company's emissions too costly, they can buy excess reductions from a facility where reductions are less expensive. The bigger the market, the theory goes, the greater the likelihood that efficiencies will be found.

By aggregating information about the value of carbon allowances, the market is sending signals to potential polluters. In today's European emissions market, for instance, emitting 1 ton of CO_2 has in the past cost polluters anywhere from under 7€ to 30€ (Hamilton, 2006). In a world where pollution has no price, the default decision will always be to pollute. In a world where pollution costs between 7€ and 30€ a ton, the decision is no longer quite so easy. Polluters suddenly must consider a new suite of options: do they accept the cost of added pollution, change fuel mixes or simply conserve energy?

Once markets take shape, emitters have a variety of options available to them. If they believe they can reduce emissions cheaply by changing production processes or experimenting with new technology, they have an incentive to do so. If they believe they can change their production process, but that this will take time, emitters can purchase credits up front in the hopes that, down the line, they will be able to make them back through emissions reduction technologies. If, on the other hand, emitters believe they will emit more in the long run, they can buy credits now (or options on credits once secondary markets develop) for use later. In short, the system enables the trading of emissions across temporal as well as geographic boundaries, a basic benefit of markets.

The market-based approach also allows other third-party players, such as speculators, to enter the fray. By agreeing to take on market risks in exchange for possible paybacks, speculators assume the risks that others are either unwilling or unable to shoulder. Other interested parties also can get involved. If, for example, an environmental group wants to see emissions decrease below a regulated target, they can raise money to buy and retire emissions allowances. This drives up the cost of emissions and can force utilities to become more efficient.

It is, of course, important to note that some people dispute the net gain of such benefits, and others feel that markets allow companies to 'greenwash' previously tarnished environmental reputations without changing their behaviour in important ways. 'Carbon offsets are based on fictitious carbon accounting, and can by themselves not make a company carbon neutral', argues Larry Lohmann of The Corner House, the UK based non-governmental organization (NGO). 'The practice of offsetting is slowing down innovation at home and abroad and diverting attention away from the root causes of climate change.' (Wright, 2006).

This debate notwithstanding, experimentation with environmental markets is now widespread. Ever since the US established the first large-scale environmental market (to regulate emissions of gases that lead to acid rain), we have seen environmental markets emerging to trade in everything from wetlands to woodpeckers.

Carbon markets

The term *carbon market* refers to the buying and selling of emissions permits that have been either distributed by a regulatory body or generated by GHG emission reductions projects. Six GHGs are generally included in 'carbon' markets: CO_2, methane, nitrous oxide, sulfur hexafluoride, hydro fluorocarbons and perfluorocarbons.

GHG emission reductions are traded in *carbon credits*, which represent the reduction of GHGs equal to one metric ton of CO_2 (tCO_2e), the most common GHG. A group of scientists associated with the Intergovernmental Panel on Climate Change (IPCC) has determined the global warming potential (GWP) of each gas in terms of its equivalent in tons of carbon dioxide (i.e. tCO_2e) over the course of 100 years. For example, the GHG methane has a GWP roughly 23 times higher than CO_2, hence one ton of methane equals about 23 tCO_2e. Likewise, other gases have different equivalences in terms of tCO_2e, some of them (perfluorocarbons) are worth thousands of tons of CO_2e.

GHG emissions reduction credits can be accrued through two different types of transactions. In *project-based transactions*, emissions credits are the result of a specific carbon offset project. *Allowance-based transactions* involve the trading of issued allowances created and allocated by regulators under a cap-and-trade regime. In cap-and-trade, the regulatory authority caps the quantity of emissions that participants are permitted to emit and issues a number of tradable allowance units equal to the cap. Participants who reduce their emissions internally beyond required levels can sell unused allowances to other participants at whatever price the market will bear.

Carbon markets can be separated into two major categories: the compliance (or regulatory) and voluntary markets. Because the voluntary market inherently does not operate under a universal cap, all carbon credits purchased in the voluntary market are project-based transactions (the exception here is the Chicago Climate Exchange).

Box 1.2 The Chicago Climate Exchange (CCX)

Richard Sandor, a former chief economist at the Chicago Board of Trade, launched, 'North America's only voluntary, legally binding rules-based greenhouse gas emission reduction and trading system' in 2003 (www.chicagoclimatex.com/). He called the trading platform the Chicago Climate Exchange (CCX).

The exchange refers to the carbon credits it trades as carbon financial instruments (CFIs, also measured in tCO_2e) and restricts trading to members who have voluntarily signed up to its mandatory reductions policy. During the pilot phase (2003–2006) members agreed to reduce greenhouse gas emissions 1 per cent a year from a baseline determined by their average emissions during 1998 to 2001 (see www.chicagoclimatex.com/). The current goal (Phase II) is for members to reduce their total emissions by 6 per cent below the baseline by 2010. Hence, members who have been participating for the past four years only need to reduce an additional 2 per cent, while new members need to reduce 6 per cent during this time (Hamilton, 2006).

Like the carbon market in general, CCX trades six different types of GHGs converted to tCO_2e. Unlike most of the voluntary carbon market, the majority of trading on CCX is allowance based, rather than project based. In other words, CCX operates as a cap-and-trade system in which members agree to cap emissions at a stated level and then trade allowances with other participants if they are either under or over their target. While CCX allows members to invest in offset projects as a means of meeting emissions targets, just 1/50th of the transactions taking place on the exchange are for CFIs generated through offset projects (Walsh, 2006). The majority of the credits are allowance-based credits, created by member companies internally reducing their emissions. When and where offset projects are used, CCX requires that an approved third party organization verify that the project's emissions reductions are real and that they meet standards set by the exchange.

Since its launch in late 2003, CCX has grown in membership from 19 institutions to over 131 institutions. Ford Motor, International Paper, IBM, American Electric Power, the City of Chicago, the City of Portland, the City of Oakland, the State of New Mexico, the World Resources Institute and the Rocky Mountain Institute are just a few of its wide range of members from the business, governmental and philanthropic sectors. CCX traded 1.45 million tCO_2e in 2005 for a total value of US$2.7 million. The average weighted price per tCO_2e in 2005 was US$1.95. Trading prices spiked in the first quarter of 2006 to US$5.00 when post-2006 vintages were announced and – according to sources – a US Senator began openly speculating that the US. might someday adopt CCX as its de-facto carbon-trading scheme. The first quarter of 2006 also saw higher trading volumes, with a total US$1.25 million exchanged (Capoor and Ambrosi, 2006).

In 2005, CCX created the European Carbon Exchange (ECX), a wholly-owned subsidiary which has since become the largest exchange trading carbon credits on the EU Emission Trading Scheme (see below). And CCX announced the creation of three new exchanges in 2006: the Montreal Climate Exchange (MCX), the Northeastern Climate Exchange (NECX), and the New York Climate Exchange (NYCX). These initiatives are presumably designed to interface with carbon credit schemes in Canada and with the Regional Greenhouse Gas Initiative (RGGI) in the US Northeast.

Compliance carbon markets

There are now a number of regulated cap-and-trade carbon markets around the world. The Kyoto Protocol underpins in one way or another most of these markets, although it is directly concerned only with the biggest of them. Ratified by 163 countries, the Protocol is a legally binding treaty committing industrialized countries to reduce their collective GHGs by 5.4 per cent below 1990 levels by 2012. The Kyoto Protocol's authors created three major 'flexibility mechanisms' in order to provide the treaty's signatories with a cost-effective means of achieving their greenhouse gas emission reduction targets. These mechanisms are the basis for the regulated international compliance carbon market:

- Emissions trading: An allowance-based transaction system that enables countries with emissions targets to purchase carbon credits from one another in order to fulfill their Kyoto commitments.
- Joint Implementation (JI): A project-based transaction system that allows developed countries to purchase carbon credits from greenhouse gas reduction projects implemented in another developed country or in a country with an economy in transition (specifically from the formerly communist

countries of Eastern Europe). Emissions from these JI projects are referred to as Emission Reduction Units (ERUs).

- Clean Development Mechanism (CDM): Another project-based transaction system through which industrialized countries can accrue carbon credits by financing carbon reduction projects in developing countries. Carbon offsets originating from registered and approved CDM projects take the form of Certified Emissions Reductions (CERs).

The carbon compnay analyst, Point Carbon, estimates that in 2005 buyers contracted for 397 million tons (Mt) of CO_2e under the Clean Development Mechanism (CDM) of the Kyoto Protocol (up from 14Mt in 2004). Assuming payment on delivery and a 7 per cent discount rate, they estimated that this market was worth €1.9 billion (about $2.38 billion). The other Kyoto mechanism for flexibility was believed to have traded only 28Mt of carbon, and was worth around €96 million ($120.5 million) (Point Carbon, 2006).

Beyond these direct Kyoto markets, countries have established (or are establishing) national or regional emissions trading schemes to help them meet their Kyoto targets. The largest of these schemes is the EU Emission Trading Scheme (EU ETS), which the European Union launched in January 2005 to help achieve the greenhouse gas emission reductions required of the region by the Kyoto Protocol. The EU ETS involves all of the EU's member states and allows limited trading with the three Kyoto mechanisms described above through a linking directive. More specifically, EU members may trade allowances (known as EUAs) with one another, or they may buy and sell carbon credits – ERUs and CERs – generated by Joint Implementation (JI) or Clean Development Mechanism (CDM) projects.

By the end of its first year of trading, the ETS had transacted an estimated 362 million tons (Mt) of carbon, worth approximately €7.2 billion- (or US$9 billion-) worth of carbon credits (Point Carbon, 2006; Capoor and Ambrosi, 2006). According to Point Carbon, this was up from 17Mt of forward trading the year prior).

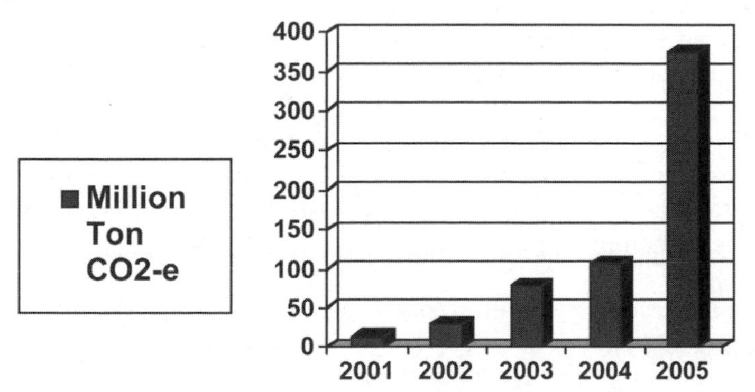

Figure 1.2 *Growth in the global carbon market*

Note: The Kyoto Protocol's entry into force and the launch of the European Union's Emission Trading Scheme drove huge expansion in the global carbon market in 2005 (Lecocq and Capoor, 2005; Capoor and Ambrosi, 2006).

Outside Europe, regulated emissions trading schemes related to the Kyoto Protocol have not developed as quickly. Japan and Canada ratified the treaty, and Japanese companies, in particular, have been active buyers of carbon credits on the CDM market, but neither country has launched a regulated emissions trading scheme of its own. The Japanese government has a government-mediated voluntary market for carbon, and Canada was in the process of setting up a scheme when there was a change of government. The current government has since said it is not sure it will meet its Kyoto targets and has talked of scrapping plans for emissions trading. The environment minister, however, has given indications that the country may seek to link up with trading schemes in the US.

The explosive growth of the global compliance carbon market under the Kyoto Protocol has meant that prices for carbon credits have been extremely volatile. Despite this volatility, the market now seems to be maturing, as regulators and participants refine their approach to allocating and trading carbon credits. A short paragraph from the World Bank's 'State and Trends of the Carbon Market 2006' report suggests the level of sophistication to which the compliance carbon market quickly evolved:

> *Financial innovation thrived as a plethora of clever carbon-based securities and hedge instruments became available to hedge carbon price risk against price volatility in other commodity markets. Brokers, consultants, carbon procurement funds, hedge fund managers and other buyers scoured the globe for opportunities to buy credits associated with projects that reduce emissions in developing countries. Innovative structures that managed both downside and upside carbon price risk and reduced delivery risk began to emerge, which aligned purchases of carbon with an interest in the underlying project through equity, debt, mezzanine finance, technology or operating agreements. The City of London developed as a sort of hub for many of these activities and a vibrant new climate services industry developed (Capoor and Ambrosi, 2006).*

Echoing the World Bank's analysis, Annie Petsonk, international counsel for Environmental Defense's Global and Regional Air Program says she is particularly pleased with some of the innovations triggered by the CDM. Inspired by the active market in Europe, Petsonk says people are now pouring money into new clean technologies in the hopes of capitalizing on a perceived first-mover advantage. Indeed, the European experience with carbon trading suggests that large-scale environmental markets not only are feasible, but also are capable of changing the way businesses relate to environmental issues (Kenny 2006).

Movement in the US

While neither Australia nor the US (two of the largest per-capita emitters of GHGs in the world) chose to ratify the Kyoto Protocol, state governments in both countries have initiated their own regulatory processes, alone or in conjunction with others.

In 1997 the US state of Oregon enacted the Oregon Standard, the first regulation of CO_2 in the US. The Oregon Standard requires that new power plants built in Oregon reduce their carbon dioxide emissions to 17 per cent below the most efficient combined cycle plant. Plants may achieve this target by offsetting their emissions through proposed offset projects or by paying mitigation funds to The Climate Trust, a non-profit organization created to implement projects that avoid or sequester CO_2 emissions. Since its creation, The Climate Trust has offset more than 1.6 million metric tons of carbon dioxide. The organization has a portfolio of over US$4 million invested in greenhouse gas offset projects, and anticipates securing an additional US$4-to-$6 million in project-based reduction in 2006 (www.climatetrust.org/).

On the East Coast of the US, eight states are developing the Regional Greenhouse Gas Initiative (RGGI), a regional strategy to reduce carbon dioxide emissions utilizing a cap-and-trade system. The programme commits participating states to cap their emissions at 1990 levels after 2009 and then drop them by 10 per cent by 2018. RGGI will cover electric utilities capable of producing at least 25 megawatts of power, giving power plants three-year compliance periods to submit one CO_2 allowance for every ton of CO_2 emitted.

The programme allows utilities to use offset projects that occur away from the power plant itself to meet emissions targets, but only on a limited basis. Initially, utilities may use offset projects – which include capturing landfill methane, planting trees and energy efficiency programmes – to cover 3.3 per cent of their emissions. If allowance prices rise beyond expected levels, then RGGI will allow utilities to use more offsets (Biello, 2006).

Importantly, the RGGI memorandum of understanding highlights an interest in expanding 'the geographic reach of the Program.' In thinking about future expansion, RGGI's architects are watching California especially closely. While California does not have any trading scheme functioning yet, the state commission charged with developing its GHG programme has expressed an interest in cap-and-trade programmes and has called for links with RGGI and the state passed landmark legislation in August 2006 in the form of a bill called AB32. The bill requires a 25% cut in the state's carbon dioxide emissions by 2020, and insiders say that cap-and-trade will, indeed, be one of the mechanisms used to reach the target. California also has one of the most highly developed registries of carbon credits (the California Climate Action Registry, or CCAR), a registry that might be mimicked not only in the US Northeast, but also in the US Midwest. If programmes on the East and West coasts link up, say carbon market experts, a national trading programme in the US, will not be far behind (Anderson, 2006).

Australia's Pioneers

While Europe's compliance carbon market clearly leads the world in terms of sophistication and scale, it is worth noting that the state of New South Wales

(NSW) in Australia launched the NSW Greenhouse Gas Abatement Scheme on January 1, 2003, two years before the first trade ever took place on the EU ETS.

The NSW Greenhouse Gas Abatement Scheme is a state-level programme designed to reduce emissions from the energy sector through carbon trading. Under the scheme, NSW energy producers may not emit any more than their apportioned share of a statewide target. Legislators set the target at 8.65 tons of carbon dioxide equivalent per capita in 2003, decreasing by about 3 per cent each year thereafter through to 2007, when it will remain at 7.27 tons (Hanley, 2006).

Under the scheme, energy producers exceeding their allotment of emissions can offset them either by surrendering NSW Greenhouse Abatement Certificates (NGACs) purchased from other producers, or by paying an $11/tonne fine. 'Prices started at about A$6 when the scheme started, but we've recently seen deals that settle early 2010 trade at A$17.10,' says Ken Edwards, a broker at Sydney-based Next Generation Energy Solutions (Hanley, 2006). Prices, say observers, are trading above the fine because operators can get tax benefits from buying GHG credits, but not from paying the fines.

'The spot price is trading lower than the fine, but the forward price is above that, so the market is anticipating that the fine will go up,' says Edwards. 'I think the government is orchestrating a steady-as-she-goes policy with the market, looking for a target of about A$20/tonne.' (Hanley, 2006).

Iemma's vision for a national approach got a lift in August 2006, when Australia's nine states and territories proposed a National Emissions Trading Scheme (NETS) aimed at putting Australia on a path to reduce emissions by 60% by 2050. The NETS Taskforce outlined a plan to introduce mandatory emission limits for stationary energy generators based on either 2000 or 1997 levels. The proposed scheme would launch in 2010.

Unfortunately, the emission reductions driven by state and regional schemes in Australia and the US are tiny compared to those mandated by the Kyoto Protocol, and the emission reductions driven by the Kyoto Protocol are tiny compared to those scientists deem necessary. Throw in other non-market-based reduction strategies around the world and Mark Kenber, head of policy strategy at The Climate Group in London, says, 'The policies that we see around the world are nowhere near what the science suggests we need.'

Thin end of the wedge

Guy Brasseur, head of the Hamburg-based Max Planck Institute for Meteorology, echoed Kenber's comments when he told the European Parliament in November of 2005, 'Kyoto won't be enough.'

'Emissions,' said Brasseur, 'will need to fall by 80 or 90 per cent, rather than five or 10 per cent, to have an effect on the models. In terms of a response, Kyoto is only a start.' (Kenny, 2006).

In the absence of a much larger global effort to reduce GHG emissions, models suggest the amount of CO_2 trapped in the atmosphere will double within the next 50 years and quadruple by the turn of the century. According to Professor Steve Pacala, head of Princeton University's Carbon Mitigation Initiative, that would 'bring out the monsters behind the door' – melting the Greenland ice cap, washing away coastal cities, spreading famine, and inter-mixing hurricanes with prolonged droughts (Kenny, 2006).

While scientists cannot say how many gigatons of CO_2 emitted into the atmosphere will produce how many degrees of warming, they do agree that roughly seven billion tons – seven gigatons – of CO_2 emissions must be prevented from entering the atmosphere during the next 50 years in order to stabilize the concentration of CO_2 in the atmosphere at 500ppm. Pacala slices a metaphorical emissions pie into seven wedges in order to demonstrate how the world might achieve a seven-gigaton cut (Pacala and Socolow, 2004). With each slice representing one gigaton of carbon dioxide emissions, Western Europe's emissions comprise about one wedge of the pie. In other words, if the ETS meets its current targets and then extends them for the next four decades, it would remove one slice of the pie (Kenny, 2006).

The current carbon market, it seems, represents only the very thin end of the wedge when it comes to combating climate change. Fortunately, however, wedges sometimes work like levers. Recognizing the need for increased action, some institutions and individuals have undertaken voluntary commitments to minimize (or even neutralize) their contribution to climate change by offsetting their emissions through investments in projects that either remove an equivalent amount of carbon dioxide from the atmosphere, or prevent it from being emitted in the first place.

Much like the credits traded in a regulated cap-and-trade scheme, voluntary offset projects generate credits equal to the removal or avoided emission of one ton of carbon dioxide. Institutions voluntarily purchasing credits either have set caps on themselves, such as 10 per cent reductions below 1990 levels, or have decided to offset some or all of the emissions related to their activities. Institutions claiming to have offset their greenhouse gas emissions must retire credits purchased. As in a compliance market, carbon credits in a voluntary market ideally allow actors to reduce emissions at least cost.

Voluntary carbon market

Voluntary carbon markets are nothing new; in fact, they pre-date all regulated carbon markets. The world's first carbon offset deal was brokered in 1989 (long before the Kyoto Protocol was signed, let alone ratified), when AES Corp., an American electricity company, invested in an agro-forestry project in Guatemala (Hawn, 2005).

Since trees use and store carbon as they grow (an example of carbon sequestration), AES reasoned it could offset the GHGs it emitted during electricity production by paying farmers in Guatemala to plant 50 million pine and eucalyptus trees on their land (Hawn, 2005). AES, like other companies since, hoped to reduce its 'carbon footprint' for philanthropic and marketing reasons, not because it was forced to do so by legislation or global treaty. The deal thus was voluntary, marking the beginning of a voluntary carbon market that remains as controversial and interesting today as it was in 1989.

Unlike the regulated market, the voluntary market does not rely on legally mandated reductions to generate demand. As a result, the market suffers from fragmentation and a lack of widely available impartial information. The fragmented and opaque nature of the voluntary market can, in large part, be attributed to the fact that it is partially composed of deals that are negotiated on a case-by-case basis, and that many of these deals neither require the carbon credits to undergo a uniform certification or verification process nor register them with any central body. As a result, there are many types of carbon transactions on the voluntary market and a variety of businesses and non-profits based on different models sell a range of products, certified to a wide array of standards.

The lack of uniformity, transparency and registration in the voluntary market has won it a great deal of criticism from some environmentalists who claim that it is a game of smoke and mirrors rather than an engine of actual environmental progress. Many buyers also say they are wary of the voluntary carbon market since transactions often carry real risks of non-delivery. Some companies buying carbon credits also fear that they will be criticized by NGOs if the carbon they are buying isn't seen to meet the highest possible standards.

Of concern to environmentalists and buyers, alike, is the fact that the voluntary carbon market's lack of regulation may mean it cannot reach the scale necessary to impact the problem. Because it lacks a regulatory driver, demand for credits can be volatile and fickle. The sudden explosion of the Kyoto carbon market in 2005 shows the difference that regulation can make. Clearly, regulation is key to driving large-scale demand. 'The voluntary credit market could grow by an order of magnitude or two orders of magnitude and it's still not going to impact the problem,' explains Mark Trexler, president of Trexler Climate & Energy Services (Trexler, 2006).

Despite the shortcomings of the voluntary market, many feel it is a fast-evolving arena with some distinct and important advantages over the regulated carbon market. While the wide range of products emerging from the voluntary market can be confusing to potential buyers, these products can also be highly innovative and flexible. Numerous suppliers say they benefit from this flexibility and the lower transaction costs associated with it.

For example, the cost of getting a carbon offset project approved by the CDM Executive Board under the Kyoto Protocol ranges anywhere from US$50,000 to US$250,000 (Krolik, 2006). By the time the United Nations CDM Executive Board finally registers a typical small-scale CDM project (essentially creating the CER that can be sold on the CDM markets), the United Nations Development Programme (UNDP) calculates that the project's total up-front costs will account for 14–22 per cent of the net present value of its revenue from carbon credits (Krolik, 2006). For many projects, coming up with the start-up capital to register a project for the compliance carbon market is prohibitively difficult.

The voluntary carbon markets, on the other hand, don't have these sorts of transaction costs. They can avoid 'bottlenecks' in the CDM methodology approval process and get carbon financing for methodologies that aren't currently 'approved' for sale by the CDM process. For example, the Nature Conservancy is working towards obtaining carbon financing for forest protection projects (what in Kyoto parlance is referred to as 'avoided deforestation'), a concept not currently approved to produce carbon credits within the CDM process.

The innovation, flexibility and lower transaction costs of the voluntary carbon market can benefit buyers as well as suppliers. When an organization purchases carbon offsets to meet a public relations or branding need, creativity, speed, cost-effectiveness and the ability to support specific types of projects (e.g. those that also benefit local communities or biodiversity) can often be clear and valuable benefits.

Having weighed such pros and cons, many non-profit organizations are supportive of the voluntary carbon market because it provides individuals – not just corporations and large organizations – with a means of participating in the fight against climate change in a way that the compliance markets do not. And since individuals account for most of the GHG emissions currently being put into the atmosphere (more than 50 per cent by some counts; Biello, 2006), some environmentalists view the voluntary carbon market as an important tool for educating the public about climate change and their potential role in addressing the problem.

Last but not least, some sellers and buyers of carbon credits prefer the voluntary carbon market precisely because it does not depend on regulation. As the international political community struggles to implement an effective climate-change framework, the voluntary carbon market has the potential to become an active driver of change today.

A more formal affair

Be they fans or critics, experts agree that the voluntary carbon market is in a critical period right now. Spurred by the success of the regulated carbon markets, the voluntary market is formalizing, as investors who cut their teeth on the regulated market look for other places to put their money, and as buyers and sellers consolidate around a few guiding practices and business models from which conclusions can be drawn about market direction and opportunities.

Although nobody has exact numbers on the size of the voluntary carbon market, most think it has grown rapidly in the last two years. Kenber of The Climate Group gives the following estimates of past and projected market size:

Table 1.1 *Voluntary carbon market size*

Year	Estimated/projected market volume (million tons/yr)
2004	3–5Mt
2005	10–20Mt
2006	20–50Mt
2007	100Mt

Source: Kenber, 2006

While maturing quickly, the voluntary market remains relatively small. Kenber's outside estimate that 20Mt of carbon may have traded on the voluntary carbon market last year is probably optimistic. And to put this number in perspective, 20Mt traded on the EU ETS in a single week in April 2006. Despite the comparatively small scale of the voluntary carbon market, some investors believe it is poised for explosive growth and some companies see real business opportunities associated with the creation of carbon-neutral products for retail consumption. If these predictions are to be borne out, most market players think it will be necessary to formalize and streamline the voluntary market, making it more accessible and gaining the confidence of large institutional buyers in Australia, Europe, Asia and North America.

At present there are several related and unrelated efforts underway to make the voluntary carbon market more 'investor-friendly' by creating registries, documenting the size of the market, and standardizing the credits being sold.

For instance, the World Business Council for Sustainable Development (WBCSD) and the World Resources Institute (WRI) jointly issued the Greenhouse Gas Protocol for Project Accounting (WBCSD/WRI GHG Protocol) in December 2005. In March of 2006, the International Organisation for Standardisation (ISO) followed up with the ISO 14064 standards for greenhouse gas accounting and verification. According to an ISO press release, these standards are intended to:

- promote consistency, transparency and credibility in GHG quantification, monitoring, reporting and verification;
- enable organizations to identify and manage GHG-related liabilities, assets and risks;
- facilitate the trade of GHG allowances or credits; and
- support the design, development and implementation of comparable and consistent GHG schemes or programmes.

Several other, related initiatives include: the Voluntary Carbon Standard (VCS), which is still in its formative stages, and the Gold Standard for Voluntary Emission Reductions (GSV), which was released in May 2006.

The Bank of New York, meanwhile, has launched a global registrar and custody service to facilitate trading of voluntary carbon credits following the

VCS. According to the bank, the new service will allow buyers and sellers to transfer voluntary carbon credits in a centralized, secure and paperless environment. 'We expect our collective efforts will greatly assist in the development of this important market,' says Karen Peetz, senior executive vice president and head of The Bank of New York's Corporate Trust Division (Bank of New York, 2006).

Whatever one's take on the long term prospects of the voluntary carbon market, it seems clear that, in the short term, the market is evolving quickly, creating new economic and environmental opportunities for investors, businesses, non-profits and individuals. It is therefore important to understand how this market operates. In the next chapter, then, we will turn our attention to addressing a basic but all-important question: how does the voluntary carbon market really work?

References

Anderson, C. (2006) 'California at the forefront', *The Ecosystem Marketplace,* www.ecosystemmarketplace.com/

Bank of New York Company (2006) 'The Bank of New York creates global registrar and custody service for voluntary carbon units', *Business Wire Inc.*

Biello, D. (2006) 'Eight is not enough', *The Ecosystem Marketplace,* www.ecosystemmarketplace.com/

Biello, D. (2006) 'A drive to offset emissions', *The Ecosystem Marketplace,* www.ecosystemmarketplace.com/

Capoor, K. and Ambrosi, P. (2006) *State and Trends of the Carbon Market 2006,* The World Bank, Washington, DC

Hamilton, K. (2006) 'Navigating a nebula: Institutional use of the U.S. voluntary carbon market,' Masters Thesis at the Yale School of Forestry and Environmental Studies

Hanley, M. (2006) 'Hitting the target: NSW producers meet compliance deadline in trading scheme', *The Ecosystem Marketplace,* www.ecosystemmarketplace.com/

Hawn, A. (2004) 'Don't wait until "day after tomorrow" to solve fossil fuel emissions problem', *St. Paul Pioneer Press,* Distributed by Knight Ridder, St. Paul, Minnesota

Hawn, A. (2005) 'Horses for courses – Voluntary vs. CDM carbon projects in Mexico', *The Ecosystem Marketplace,* www.ecosystemmarketplace.com/

Kenber, M. (2006) 'Raising the Bar for Voluntary Environmental Credit Markets', Presentation at GreenT Forum New York, 2–3 May, 2006

Kenny, A. (2006) 'The thin end of the wedge', *The Ecosystem Marketplace,* www.ecosystemmarketplace.com/

Krolik, T. (2006) 'The Argentine Carbon Fund Helps Developers Dance the Dance', *The Ecosystem Marketplace,* www.ecosystemmarketplace.com/

Lecocq, F. and Capoor, K. (2005) *State and Trends of the Carbon Market 2005,* The World Bank, Washington D.C.

Linden, E. (2006) *The Winds of Change,* Simon & Schuster, New York

Pacala, S. and Socolow, R. (2004) 'Stabilization wedges: solving the climate problem for the next 50 years with current technologies', *Science* (August 2004: pp968–972)

Point Carbon (2006), 'Carbon 2006: towards a truly global market'. H. Hasselknippe & K Roine eds

Trexler, M. (2006) Presentation at GreenT Forum: Raising the Bar for Voluntary Environmental Credit Markets. New York, 2–3 May
Walsh, M. (2006) Presentation at GreenT Forum: Raising the Bar for Voluntary Environmental Credit Markets. New York, 2–3 May
Wright, C. (2006) 'Carbon Neutrality Draws Praise, Raises Expectations for HSBC', *The Ecosystem Marketplace*, www.ecosystemmarketplace.com/

2

Understanding Supply and Demand in the Voluntary Carbon Market

In December 2004 one of the world's largest banks, HSBC, surprised many observers by announcing it had decided to make its operations carbon neutral. What surprised people wasn't so much that the bank had agreed to take the issue of climate change seriously, but that it had – voluntarily – agreed to spend millions of dollars over the next ten years to minimize its contribution to the problem. As a dry run, HSBC put out a tender for projects that would offset 170,000tCO_2e emitted by the bank during the last quarter of 2005. More than 100 emission reduction projects responded to HSBC's request, and the company was able to shortlist 17 based on criteria related to project size, technology employed, country and vintage. When all was said and done, the company spent some US$750,000 buying offsets from a handful of projects in Germany, India, Australia and New Zealand (HSBC, 2005). But the process was a steep learning curve for the bank, which led environment adviser, Francis Sullivan to conclude: 'We need a better way of finding what we want in the market.' (The Climate Group, 2005).

Sullivan's statement encapsulates both the challenges and opportunities in the voluntary carbon market. Institutions buying and selling voluntary carbon offsets face a fragmented market, a complex supply chain, and a lack of consistent standards. Each new 'climate neutral' product offering or company seems to employ a different business strategy for achieving its carbon goals, while carbon credit providers source offsets through an array of projects that range from planting trees in Australia to installing solar systems in Bangladeshi villages to capturing methane in American landfills. Hence, the market operates under the principle of *caveat emptor*: let the buyer beware.

There are signs, however, that the market is beginning to consolidate around a few guiding practices and business models from which conclusions can be drawn about market direction and opportunities. This chapter attempts to help institutions assess these evolving opportunities by looking at the intricacies of supply and demand in the voluntary carbon market.

A look at the supply chain

Institutions and individuals acquire offsets in a number of ways, but a simplified model of the voluntary carbon market's supply chain includes the following elements: a project or project idea is generated, the resulting emission reductions are verified to some standard to create carbon credits, the credits are sold to middlemen, and the middlemen sell them on to businesses and individuals (Figure 2.1). Brokers and exchanges may assist in the distribution of offsets by facilitating transactions between buyers and sellers, but they usually do not buy or sell credits.

In some cases, project developers may skip stage two and/or three of this sequence, selling either verified or unverified credits directly to consumers. The International Small Group and Tree Planting Alliance (TIST), for instance, has sold verified offsets generated by subsistence farmers in East Africa and India directly to individual consumers via a virtual 'store' on eBay (Hawn, 2005).

Stage 1: product creation

In most cases, project development is the first step in the supply chain for carbon credits destined for the voluntary carbon market. It is worth noting, however, that some projects start simply as a concept or idea and may not begin until a buyer supplies funding.

In theory, a single landowner might develop a project on his or her land and sell the resulting offsets directly to a buyer. In practice, project developers are usually: non-profit organizations interested in combating climate change and/or contributing to sustainable development; private companies (e.g. timber companies) that are uniquely positioned to develop projects; small private-sector companies that have been set up in response to the carbon market; or public sector agencies interested in seeding the market. The bottom line, then, is that project developers come in all stripes and sizes.

Similarly, while the term, carbon credit, implies a uniform commodity, in reality carbon offsets originate from a wide variety of project types that can differ at numerous levels. An exciting aspect of the voluntary market is that buyers can choose to provide carbon financing for specific types of projects,

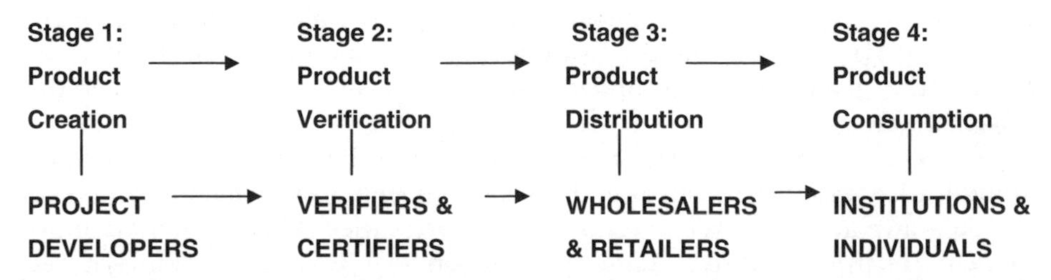

Figure 2.1 *Simplified supply chain of the retail carbon market*

and support specific co-benefits (e.g. benefits for biodiversity, or benefits for local communities), in addition to GHG reductions.

One differentiating factor is project size. CDM definitions illustrate the range of projects in the compliance and voluntary markets and categorize projects as 'small' or 'large.' CDM projects that generate less than 15 kilotons of carbon dioxide annually are placed in the small project category and all others are placed in the large project category (see www.cdm.unfccc.int/). For the majority of project developers 'big is beautiful,' and large projects have dominated the regulatory and voluntary markets to date (Clarke, 2003). The World Bank reported that, 'From 2004 to 2005–06, the average transaction size increased from 1.24 million tCO_2e to 1.90 million tCO_2e' for all project-based transactions (i.e. transactions in both voluntary and regulatory carbon markets) (Capoor and Ambrosi, 2006). Through economies of scale, large projects often reduce transaction costs per credit, result in more GHG mitigation, and give rise to lower prices and higher profits.

In addition to being classified as either small or large, offset projects can be categorized by project type and two major levels: those reducing GHG emissions at the source and those reducing GHG levels in the atmosphere through sequestration (see Table 2.1). For a more detailed description of the different kinds of offset projects and some of their respective advantages and disadvantages see Appendix 1.

Stage 2: product verification and certification

Verification, the second stage in the supply chain, begins the life cycle of creating a product recognized by the market. While credits originating from CDM projects are often referred to as CERs, offset credits in the voluntary market are often referred to as Verified Emission Reductions (VERs). This term – sometimes used as a de facto currency in the voluntary carbon market – embodies the ideal of legitimate third party verification. Quantifying and verifying GHG emission reductions requires significant technical expertise, and monitoring throughout the project life span. Accounting questions include issues such as how many years the project is expected to generate emission reductions, the 'payback time' of various technologies (it has been estimated a 60kW photovoltaic array must produce electricity for 3.7 years before it is carbon-neutral) (Murray and Petersen, 2004), and the amount of GHG destroyed, displaced or stored.

A wide variety of accounting methods are used to establish carbon credits in the voluntary market. Some are self developed by project managers and others by a third-party verifier. Regardless of the system chosen, a few major issues usually guide considerations of offset quality (Hamilton, 2006):

- Additionality – The project must be additional to a business-as-usual scenario and there must be some assurance that the project would not occur without the funding provided by carbon credits. (For more on additionality, see Box 2.1).

Table 2.1 *Project types generating carbon credits for the voluntary carbon market*

	Advantages	***Disadvantages***
Methane capture from landfills	– Efficient means of reducing emissions – Captured methane can be used as fuel – Few leakage concerns – Somewhat reduced odours – Reduced risk of ground water contamination – Relatively inexpensive	– Additionality concerns should be carefully considered
Methane capture from livestock	– Efficient means of reducing emissions – Captured methane can be used as fuel – Few leakage concerns – Reduced odours and co-pollutants – Reduced risk of ground water contamination – Relatively inexpensive	– Additionality concerns should be carefully considered
Methane capture from coal mines	– Efficient means of reducing emissions – Captured methane can be used as fuel – Few leakage concerns – Can improve safety for mine workers – Relatively inexpensive	– Additionality concerns should be carefully considered
Industrial gas destruction	– Very efficient – Highly additional – Relatively inexpensive	– Potential supply is limited
Direct fossil fuel reduction	– Supports clean technology – Cost savings – Reduces co-pollutants (ex. Sox, PM, VOCs) – Reduces fossil fuel dependency – Potential social benefits	– Relatively inefficient means of reducing GHGs
Indirect fossil fuel reduction (RECs)	– Already established market with certification/verification systems – Supporting on-grid renewable energy important for decreasing reliance on fossil fuels – Reduces co-pollutants (ex. Sox, PM, VOCs) from fossil fuels	– Compatibility issues between markets for RECs and carbon offsets – Additionality concerns should be carefully considered
Reforestation/ Afforestation of native tree species	– Large number of potential social co-benefits – Contributes to biodiversity conservation – Addresses deforestation which is an important part of the climate change problem	– Lack of permanence – Relatively inefficient means of reducing GHGs – Less efficient than many mono-crop projects – Relatively expensive – Leakage and additionality considerations

Table 2.1 *Continued*

	Advantages	***Disadvantages***
Avoided deforestation of native tree species	– Large number of potential social co-benefits – Contributes to biodiversity conservation – Addresses deforestation which is an important part of the climate change problem	– Lack of permanence – Relatively inefficient means of reducing GHGs – Less efficient than many mono-crop projects – Relatively expensive – Additionality and leakage considerations
Monoculture forestry	– Some potential for social co-benefits – Trees with high sequestration rates can be selected – Often lower cost – Deforestation part of the climate change problem	– Lack of permanence – Relatively inefficient means of reducing GHGs – Concerns about water consumption – Reduced social and environmental co-benefits compared to projects working with native tree species
Soil sequestration	– Reduced erosion – Large number of potential social co-benefits – Improved water quality – Relatively inexpensive	– Questions of additionality and permanence should be carefully considered
Geological sequestration	– Huge potential for storage – Domestic fuel source	– Enables fossil fuel use, leading to more CO_2 emissions

- Permanence – The project must be able to guarantee GHG mitigation over the stated time period. This is especially important in long-term projects, such as pre-pay reforestation in which risks such as a fire would affect the delivery of credits. Indeed, all forms of sequestration projects need to ensure that the carbon that is stored either in trees or underground will not some day be released into the atmosphere.
- Leakage – The project must not transfer emissions to another location outside the project area. Leakage occurs when emissions reductions at one site or point of time, indirectly drive increased emissions from another activity outside of the project boundary. For example, if a forestry project limits logging in one area, developers should consider the possibility that deforestation will simply occur elsewhere.

- Double Counting – The project must avoid double counting its emissions reductions. Double counting can occur when more than one organization takes credit for owning or retiring offsets. Accurate and publicly available inventories can help resolve this problem. For example, direct and indirect emissions should be inventoried and reported separately.
- Ex-ante & Ex-post Accounting – In ex-ante accounting credits are sold before they are produced; in ex-post accounting they are sold after. The former entail more risk, command lower prices and require stringent guarantees.
- Co-Benefits – While the primary goal of carbon credits is to offset GHGs, many types of projects provide additional benefits, such as reductions of other pollutants, contributions to local communities, or habitat for biodiversity. Co-benefits range dramatically between project types, but are an important factor for many institutions purchasing emissions voluntarily. Co-benefits may also represent additional revenue streams for investors. Electricity sales, sales of other pollution credits or timber all represent financial co-benefits. It is important, however, that customers understand which co-benefits have been parceled off and which will remain 'bundled' with the carbon offset.

Most project developers finance the verification of their carbon emissions reductions before selling them to either middlemen or end-consumers in the voluntary market. In general, buyers prefer third-party verification to in-house verification for reasons of credibility. For examples of major verifiers see Appendix 2.

When a project's offsets have been verified in accordance with a particular set of certification standards and endorsed by the organization issuing the standards, it is common to say that the resulting carbon credits have been certified. In the Kyoto market, certified emissions reductions (CERs) refer to carbon credits that have been approved by the CDM executive board. Certification in the voluntary market is a more general term suggesting that an institution with a recognized set of standards has endorsed the credits in question with a stamp of approval.

In response to the high transaction costs and confusion caused by the wide range of offerings in the voluntary market, several organizations have developed standards or certification programmes. Certification could be an extremely beneficial tool to ensure a consistent level of quality, reduce transaction costs for buyers and build consumer trust. To date, however, discord surrounding the large number and variety of certification programmes in the market has caused some confusion among buyers. Table 2.2 lists some of the standards and certification programmes available for voluntary carbon credits; see Appendix 3 for more information on any of the standards listed.

Stage 3: product distribution

Once credits have been verified and/or certified, middlemen often step in either as buyers interested in purchasing credits for on-sale, or as facilitators

Table 2.2 *Major certification programmes/standards available or soon to be available for the voluntary carbon offset market*

CCB Standards	The CCB Standard was created to support land management projects that sequester GHG, support sustainable development, and conserve biodiversity.
CCX	CCX sets standards for the listing of credits (including those from offset projects) on their exchange, including the requirement of a CCX approved third party verifier.
Climate Neutral Network	The Climate Neutral Network functions as a hybrid between a consultant, certifier and retailer, branding products and companies with its Climate Cool logo.
Green-e	Green-e is the most widely accepted certifier of RECs in the US and is currently creating a third party verification standard for RECs as carbon offsets.
ISO 14064 Standard	The goal of this standard is 'to provide a set of unambiguous and verifiable requirements' for projects of all kinds.
Voluntary Carbon Standard	The VCS aims to provide a basic quality threshold for all carbon credits on the voluntary market.
Voluntary Gold Standard	The Gold Standard seeks to define quality for the high-end market of carbon credits.
WRI/WBCSD Protocol	Unlike the other standards described the WRI/ WBCSD GHG Protocol is an accounting guide that does not certify offsets or organizations. However, the Protocol now plays a major role in setting guidelines for GHG reporting.

Note: See Appendix 3 for complete list of information sources used.

interested in arranging transactions between buyers and sellers on a fee-for-service basis.

Retailers and carbon fund managers generally select and maintain investments in a portfolio of projects that generate credits over time. Like wine, credits thus have vintage years denoting the year in which they were generated. For example a project that started in 2005 and will last for three years may be able to sell credits for 2005, 2006 and 2007 vintages, or in bulk for the lifespan of the project (for example purchasing a tree that will offset emissions over its 70-year lifespan).

Retailers

An international survey of retailers, by the HWWI Research programme on Climate Policy, estimated that there were about 30–40 retail providers (some

Box 2.1 The Additionality Debate

In order to create offsets the emission reductions associated with a project must be additional to that which might be expected under a business-as-usual model. This is important because a real GHG emission is being 'allowed' into the atmosphere for each offset retired. If the offsets are not additional – if they would have happened anyway – then the net effect on the atmosphere when they are used to neutralize other emissions is negative.

While the concept of additionality is simple, implementing it is not. Debates around additionality have been considered pivotal to the integrity of various sources of carbon credits and the market as a whole (Trexler *et al.*, 2006). While most stakeholders agree that the goal of the market is to reduce total GHGs in the atmosphere, the different perspectives on how this is best accomplished are most acutely illustrated in the additionality and quality debates.

An important concept for most additionality requirements is what is considered to be the *baseline*: the 'hypothetical description of what would have most likely occurred in the absence of any considerations about climate change mitigation.' (www.ghgprotocol.org/). In order to establish that a GHG offset project has reduced emissions beyond those expected in the baseline, a variety of 'tests' for additionality are used. Five tests are outlined by the World Resources Institute (WRI) /World Business Council for Sustainable (WBCSD) Development Greenhouse Gas Protocol for Project Accounting, a widely accepted standard for project accounting.

- *Investment*: This is perhaps the most-used test. To meet it, developers must prove that potential revenue from the sale of carbon credits was a decisive reason for implementing a project that otherwise would not have happened.
- *Technology*: In order to pass the technology test for additionality, developers must show that the primary benefit derived from the technology used was a reduction of GHG emissions.
- *Regulatory*: The test for regulatory additionality requires that a project reduce emissions below the level required by law.
- *Common Practice*: Similarly, developers must prove that the project reduces GHG emissions more than similar 'business as usual' projects.
- *Timing*: Some standards require developers to demonstrate that they initiated their project after a specific date. The idea is that the timing of a project can help determine whether or not it was undertaken with the expectation of carbon financing.

Project developers and policy-makers debate which tests should be 'The Tests' in the voluntary market. The WRI/WBCSD Protocol states:

'setting the stringency of additionality rules involves a balancing act.' (www.ghgprotocol.org/). For example, additionality criteria that are too lenient may undermine the GHG programme's effectiveness. Conversely, overly stringent criteria could place burdensome limitations on creating valid GHG emissions, potentially excluding otherwise worthy project activities.

Since there is no 'technically correct' answer to the question of additionality, opinions on the ideal stringency of additionality in the voluntary market range dramatically. Many practitioners argue that additionality is not a critical factor at this stage in the development of carbon markets and that the key goal should be to create financial incentives for reducing GHGs. Some would add that the additionality argument is actually counter productive and that excessive concerns about additionality are reducing the effectiveness of the market by increasing gridlock on the path to establishing effective trading frameworks. The benefit of the voluntary market, some argue, is that it provides an arena where projects can be stimulated without passing strict additionality requirements. For example, Toby Janson-Smith, director of the Climate, Community & Biodiversity Alliance, argues that standard additionality tests exclude some of the best projects from an environmental and sustainable development perspective – namely, projects that are good for the climate, good for biodiversity, and good for local communities (Janson-Smith, 2006).

Others feel that specific additionality tests are an essential piece of developing credibility in the market and argue that strict adherence to high standards is especially important in a market where organizations and individuals are trusting that the money they've used to purchase offsets will make a difference on the ground. Moreover, proponents of carefully considering additionality, such as Trexler of Trexler Climate + Energy Services, note that because the US' voluntary market is so small, it's demand could be met by 'false positive' or non-additional offsets, leaving little incentive for investing in truly additional offsets. If consumers can't tell the difference between offsets, they'll purchase the less expensive choice, 'But you can't get real, additional GHG offsets for $1/ton.' (Trexler, 2006).

for-profit, some not-for-profit) in the world in 2005 (Butzengeiger, 2005). Most retailers work on a 'pay-as-you-go' cycle in which they maintain a small inventory of credits and 'top up' when new clients provide funding.

While a retailer's project portfolio may change over time, its transparency to consumers, together with the stringency and standards it uses when selecting projects, is what allows for product differentiation. Project portfolios often include emissions reductions projects and sequestration projects, but it is worth noting that many retailers choose to work only with emissions reductions projects or only with sequestration projects. Of those that work with both, research in late 2005 suggests that typically 80 per cent of credits are from emissions reductions projects and 20 per cent are from sequestration projects (New Forests, 2005). For a list of retailers see Appendix 4.

Investors

Unlike the regulated carbon markets where institutional investors abound, few funds currently invest in the voluntary carbon market. Climate Wedge Ltd. started the Cheyne Climate Wedge Fund, the world's first voluntary carbon offset fund, with London-based Cheyne Capital Management in July 2005. The fund seeks out and manages high-quality offsets for CO_2 emissions for large-scale corporate and institutional buyers. Climate Wedge may be the first of many hedge funds and other capital market tools to bring major speculative investment into the voluntary carbon market.

Brokers

Brokers work to facilitate transactions between institutions and offset project developers. Most frequently, brokers match buyers and sellers for CERs purchased under the CDM; however in the voluntary market they can also provide trading services for VERs. Brokers generally charge a commission of roughly 7.5 per cent for their services. Brokers in the voluntary market include Natsource, CO_2e, Ecosecurites and Trexler Climate + Energy Services (Taiyab, 2006).

Exchanges & Registries

Currently, the Chicago Climate Exchange (CCX) is the only exchange trading voluntary carbon credits, and access to the exchange is restricted to members.

The Bank of New York announced in June 2006 that it has created a registry service for corporate buyers and sellers who wish to trade voluntary carbon credits via a 'centralized, secure and paperless environment.' (Bank of New York, 2006). The registry and a team of employees to support it will be based within the Bank's corporate trust services division.

The Center for Resource Solutions (known as Green-e) says it is currently creating a third party verification standard for renewable energy credits as carbon offsets and a registry for other types of offsets verified under approved third party verification standards (Kvale, 2006).

Many retailers also maintain their own registries of carbon credits that they sell into the voluntary market. For instance, MyClimate, a Zurich-based retailer of carbon credits (many sold into the voluntary market) has its own registry of carbon credits.

Last but not least, several government agencies have stepped in to provide registries for credits generated by voluntary offset projects. The United States Department of Energy, for instance, has a National Voluntary Reporting Greenhouse Gases programme, established by Section 1605(b) of the Energy

Policy Act, which is a public database that 'provides a means for organizations and individuals who have reduced their emissions to record their accomplishments and share their ideas for action.' (www.eia.doe.gov/oiaf/1605/2ndbroc.html) Organizations can report direct emissions reductions or offset projects, such as sequestration activities. (Sampson, 2006) Similar to the national 1605 (b) Voluntary Reporting programme, the state of California created the California Climate Action Registry (CCAR), a non-profit voluntary registry for emissions reductions. Sequestration activities, but only forestry projects, can be recorded in the registry. (Anderson, 2006)

Stage 4: product 'consumption'

Consumers in the voluntary carbon market may make a one-time purchase, or they may choose to work with a middleman in an ongoing relationship, receiving credits from a project or a portfolio of projects year after year. In general, carbon credits are consumed in order to offset one of four types of emissions:

Internal emissions: Companies, non-profit organizations or government agencies may purchase carbon credits in order to offset the emissions generated by their facilities and employees in the course of doing business, such as emissions from travel, energy use, manufacturing etc. These emissions are often referred to as direct emissions or internal emissions, and this type of deal probably accounted for most of the carbon credits purchased on the voluntary carbon market last year.

Example. HSBC purchased carbon offsets in order to neutralize its group-wide emissions for the last quarter of 2005. To offset the total emissions amount (170,000 tons of carbon dioxide ±5 per cent), HSBC has bought 170,000 tons of carbon offset credits from four offset projects around the world: the Te Apiti wind farm in North Island, New Zealand; an organic waste composting project in Victoria, Australia; the Sandbeiendorf agricultural methane capture project in Sandbeiendorf, Gemany; and the Vensa Biotek biomass co-generation project in Andhra Pradesh, India. 'A large-scale collective effort is going to be needed to address climate change. Governments must play their part, and help the public to make informed decisions,' says Francis Sullivan, HSBC's advisor on the environment. 'Banks should also do their bit.' (The Climate Group, 2005; HSBC, 2005).

Product life cycle emissions: Companies, to date, have been less willing to offset the emissions generated by the use of their products (known as their indirect or external emissions), but market observers expect this may change in the coming years as companies buy credits in order to develop carbon-neutral products for their customers (Molitor, 2005). Such products generally carry a price-premium and are marketed as carbon neutral in much the same way that organically produced food products are marketed as environmentally sound. Theoretically, companies could purchase offsets in order to offset their external emissions as a matter of corporate social responsibility without using them towards the certification of carbon-neutral products, but this is less likely since most companies will capitalize on a marketing opportunity when and where possible. While the use of carbon offsets to create carbon-neutral products has been limited to date, market observers expect this form of offset consumption may one day become a staple of the voluntary carbon market (Rau, 2006).

Example. BP has launched a carbon-neutral fuel product in Australia. As part of its Global Choice programme, BP offers its commercial customers the opportunity to offset some of their GHG emissions, either by paying more for an Ultimate grade gasoline that comes with a company promise to offset the emissions generated by its use, or by partnering to purchase offsets outright. BP has already neutralized more than 800,000 metric tons of GHG emissions from its Ultimate grade gasoline customers. 'We do it because we fundamentally believe that we need to tackle climate change, whether it be from our own operations or customers using our products,' says Kerryn Schrank, business advisor for future fuels at BP. 'Offsets are going to be important for the transport sector for the next 20 years or so, until we can get cleaner transport options.' (Biello, 2005).

Event emissions: In recent years, steering committees for high-profile events have elected to take events carbon-neutral through the purchase of large numbers of carbon credits. As credits become more readily available and certification programmes gain more trust in the coming years, offsetting event emissions may become common practice for many political, athletic and social events.

Example. FIFA offset the 2006 World Cup through a voluntary 100,000-ton carbon offset programme called the Green Goal Initiative. Although official figures are not public knowledge, the budget for carbon neutrality is estimated at one million euros, which comes to an average price of ten euros per ton of carbon offset (Zwick, 2006; www.myclimate.org).

Individual emissions: In contrast to the first three types of carbon credit purchases, which involve an institutional buyer purchasing large numbers of credits, the last kind of deal involves individual consumers purchasing carbon credits in order to offset their daily activities and/or travel plans. While this side of the market is small at the moment, many social sector organizations consider it the most important type of transaction, since it allows individuals to take action against climate change, thus increasing public awareness of the market.

Example. Cyd Gorman calculates the emissions from her commute to and from work using a carbon calculator and then pays Terrapass – a business that buys carbon credits and renewable energy certificates on the voluntary market and then sells them on to individual consumers – to offset them for her. 'Think of it as Kyoto for commuters,' says Dan Neil of the Los Angeles Times (Neil, 2005).

How does the market work?

While the simplified supply chain just discussed is useful in understanding how carbon credits generally get to market, it should be noted that it is difficult to depict the market properly using a linear supply chain because a single participant can occupy more than one role. Instead, the model below gives a more realistic sense of how the voluntary carbon market currently functions.

While organizations tend to offset events, activities or products via offsets purchased from retailers, major corporate commitments to carbon neutrality generally skip this step and work directly with project developers. Major examples include BP Global Choice and Cinergy who originally sourced projects (through the Commonwealth Bank and a tender process, respectively) and now maintain direct relationships (New Forests, 2005). Some of these interactions are managed through brokers, for example Meridian Energy sells credits from its Te Apiti wind farm in New Zealand to business and retailers through brokers (New Forests, 2005). Theoretically, brokers may connect all kinds of buyers and sellers at any point in the supply chain bearing credits to market. In reality, brokers very rarely work with individual consumers, who almost exclusively purchase offsets from retailers or from project developers retailing their own credits.

As previously discussed, a growing number of businesses also offer embedded carbon neutral products to end-users. Businesses can brand products as carbon neutral (either maintaining their own branding or using a certifier's branding), which ensures to customers that emissions in the product's life cycle have been offset. For example, Interface Carpet's Climate Cool Carpet is certified by the Climate Neutral Network to be carbon neutral through a project portfolio that Interface maintains.

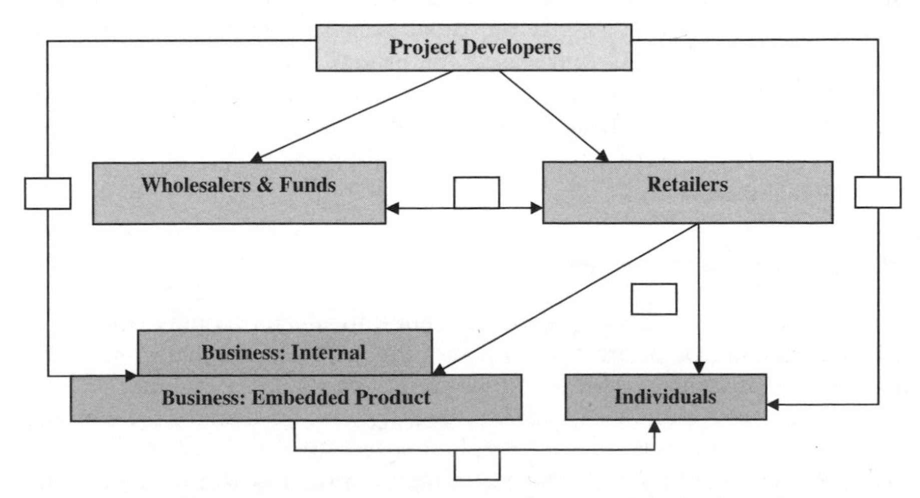

Figure 2.2 *A model of common types of transactions in the voluntary carbon market*

Price trends

Since many of the transactions in the voluntary carbon market occur over the counter and many buyers and sellers guard price information closely, it is difficult to get a bearing on the wholesale price of carbon credits.

Broadly speaking, prices can be compared at two levels: the cost of the offset project and the market price of the credit sold. Project cost is influenced by three major factors: technical reduction costs (influenced by factors such as project type, size, location, upfront costs vs. length of return, profits from co-benefits and additionality), transaction/administration costs, and seller's profit (Butzengeiger, 2005).

Market price is also influenced by several factors. For example, steps between the project and the buyer such as brokers, retail sellers, verification, certification and marketing may increase the price. Similarly, like many commodities, price often varies according to the scale of the purchase. Prices will also evolve in the voluntary market with changes in supply and demand. For example, regulation could increase the price of carbon credits in the US.

Importantly, since the attributes contributing to credit quality are only one of the factors influencing price, 'better' credits and higher prices do not always correlate. That said, 'non-additional' credits (which have little environmental value) generally cost less than other types of credits since only the transaction costs involved with claiming the credit contribute to its expense. According to the World Bank, the average-weighted price for verified emissions reductions reached US$7.20 per tCO_2e in 2005. It is important to note, however, that many of these transactions were probably for pre-compliance credits that were subsequently certified by the CDM executive board as CERs and then sold into the compliance market (Capoor and Ambrosi, 2006).

From the wholesale to the retail level, research for this book suggests voluntary credits can be found for prices ranging from less than $1.00 to as much $35.00 (New Forests, 2005). At the retail scale, a low price credit from a large-scale project can be purchased for around $4.25, while a low price credit from a smaller scale project runs at about $10.00 (Hamilton, 2006). According to the World Bank, consumers paying the highest prices for voluntary carbon credits consistently express a willingness to pay for sustainable development benefits.

What's driving the market?

Heretofore, we have made oblique reference to market drivers (the risk of future regulation, a desire for product differentiation, philanthropic aims, etc.). Now that we have a sense of how supply works in the voluntary carbon market, it is worth shining a more direct spotlight on the demand for voluntary carbon credits. Is it real? Is it robust? Is it sustainable?

Briefly, one might answer these questions, in turn, with a yes, a no and a maybe. The best way to assess these questions, however, is to look more carefully at who is buying carbon credits and why. As our earlier discussion

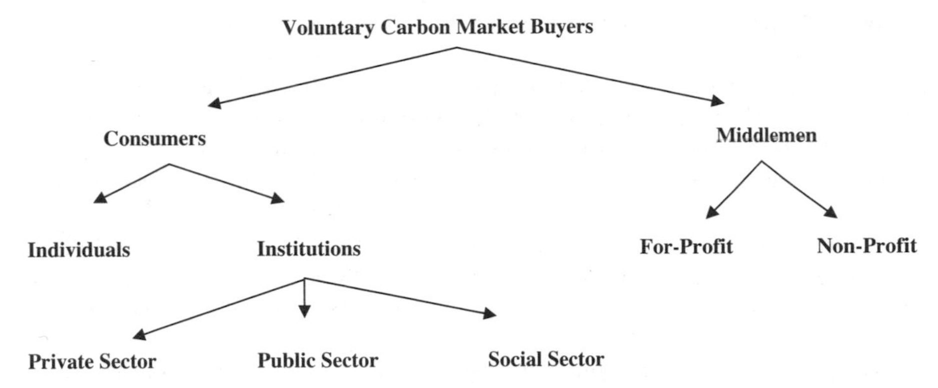

Figure 2.3 *A quick sketch of the different kinds of buyers in the voluntary carbon market*

of the supply chain revealed, there are two basic types of buyers in the voluntary carbon market: consumers and middlemen. Put simply, consumers buy credits in order to retire them to offset the emissions associated with an action, event or product. Middlemen, on the other hand, purchase credits and then sell them on to consumers without making any offset claims of their own.

Both for-profit and not-for-profit institutions act as middlemen. At the coarsest level, it is fair to say that for-profit middlemen acting as wholesalers or retailers of carbon credits are driven by profit motivations, while their not-for-profit counterparts are generally driven by environmental and sustainable development aims. It should be noted, however, that many of the for-profit organizations operating within this sphere also have philanthropic aims, but believe that a private-sector model provides the most sustainable vehicle for driving change.

Within the consumers category, one can further separate buyers into institutions and individuals. And within the institutions category, it is possible to distinguish between buyers from the private, public and social sectors.

Since it is the purchasing behavior of end-consumers that ultimately drives the market, we will look at the motivations that individual and institutional consumers have for buying carbon credits on the voluntary carbon market (i.e. the buyers listed on the left side of the above diagram). For a partial list of past buyers on the voluntary carbon market see Appendix 5.

Individual consumers

Between May and July 2006, the BBC World Service had GlobeScan and the programme on International Policy Attitudes poll 19,579 citizens across 19 countries about the world's energy use. 'People see the energy status quo as too risky,' summarizes GlobeScan President Doug Miller. 'What's fascinating is that in the midst of historically high energy prices and geopolitical tensions, the number one energy concern in every industrialized country we surveyed is the impact on environment and climate.' (Globe Scan/BBC, 2006).

With 94 per cent of those interviewed expressing concern about climate change, Australians led the world in their concern about the impact of energy policy on the environment. Brits weren't far behind at 93 per cent and 91 per cent of the Canadians and Italians interviewed also said they were concerned that current energy policies were impacting the environment adversely (GlobeScan/BBC 2006, see www.worldpublicopinion.org for full results).

Against this backdrop, it is hardly surprising that research suggests individual consumers of carbon credits on the voluntary carbon market are driven primarily by the sense that addressing climate change is the right thing to do. In the US, retailers of carbon credits say the top reason consumers cite for buying carbon credits is a desire for independence from oil (Arnold, 2006). In the UK and the rest of Europe, consumers say sustainable development concerns top the list of motivations for purchasing credits. A recent study shows that 40 per cent of European voluntary carbon purchasers would pay a premium for carbon obtained from projects with either environmental or sustainable development benefits (Taiyab, 2006).

Private sector institutions

In the absence of regulation, financial lenders and shareholder groups are pushing businesses in the US, Australia and Canada to develop strategies for managing their carbon footprint. Similarly, European companies that do not fall within the sectors currently regulated under the EU ETS (regulated sectors currently include electricity generation, oil refining, building materials, pulp and paper, and ferrous metals), are feeling increasing pressure to act on climate change (Grobbel *et al.*, 2004; http://ec.europa.eu/environment/climat/emission.htm).

The Carbon Disclosure Project (CDP), for instance, was launched six years ago by a global group of institutional investors to pressure businesses to report on their carbon emissions footprint and what they were doing to manage it. The project sends out a survey to the world's largest companies and then publishes their responses on its website. The project also publishes a list of those companies failing to respond.

Importantly, companies are beginning to respond. The first survey was sent out in 2003 and was signed by 35 institutional investors; 45 per cent of the 500 companies receiving the survey answered the questionnaire in full. By 2005, the percentage of responding companies answering the questionnaire in full had climbed to 71 per cent. 211 institutional investors representing US$31 trillion in assets signed the 2006 survey, which was sent out to 1900 companies. (http://www.cdproject.net/)

Rob Seely, general manager of sustainable development at Shell Canada, says his company views the voluntary carbon market as a risk-management tool. Specifically, the voluntary carbon market offers Shell Canada the chance to learn about carbon markets in advance of its participation in any future regulatory market, while also helping the company manage its reputation. 'We

Table 2.3 *Global sources of pressure in the private sector*

Carbon disclosure project	***Equator principles***	***UNEP finance initiative***
• 211 institutional investors representing >US$31 trillion in assets • Requests disclosure of GHG emissions from 1900 of the largest companies in the world (by market cap)	• 35 plus institutional investors (as of July 2006) accounting for a large percentage of worldwide project financing • Ensures social responsibility and environmental soundness in project financing	• Over 160 financial institutions • Promotes linkages between the environment, sustainability and financial performance

Source: Grobbel *et al*., 2004; www.cdproject.net; www.equator-principles.com/; www.unepfi.org

Table 2.4 *Regional sources of pressure in the private sector: Europe*

Institutional investors group on climate change
• 26 institutional investors/pension funds representing over US$855 billion (2004) in assets • Provides research on sectors exposed to climate change risks

Source: Grobbel *et al*., 2004; www.iigcc.org/

are part of the problem,' says Seely, 'we need to be part of the solution.' (Seely, 2006).

Amy Davidsen, director of environmental affairs at JPMorgan Chase, cites similar reasons for her institution's interest in the market: 'We really see the voluntary carbon market as an opportunity.' (Davidsen, 2006). Davidsen's assertion that companies are beginning to see action on climate change as an opportunity, not just a risk, is important because, while risk may drive a few companies to enter the carbon market, opportunity stands to attract many more. So far, the financial sector and the insurance industry seem to be out in front when it comes to structuring products and services that might allow

Table 2.5 *Regional sources of pressure in the private sector: North America*

Coalition for environmentally responsible economies (Ceres)/Investor network on climate risk (INCR)
• Members manage over US$1.3 trillion in assets • Increases financial markets' awareness of climate risks

Source: Grobbel *et al*., 2004; www.ceres.org/

them to profit from the carbon market. 'Now that carbon increasingly has a value, you can either capture it or face risk,' says Francis Sullivan, HSBC's Adviser on the Environment (Wright, 2006).

'At the stage we are now, carbon neutrality can be considered best practice in the financial sector,' says Nick Robins, head of Socially Responsible Investment (SRI) funds at Henderson Global Investors. 'Such commitments are important for building climate change literacy in the business world.' (Wright, 2006).

Henderson, hoping to understand the distribution of carbon risk across companies, recently commissioned Trucost to profile the carbon emissions of the top 100 listed companies in the UK, the FTSE 100. 'For us, the results of the Carbon 100 pointed to three critical questions for the future,' he says. 'Who owns carbon, who insures carbon, and increasingly, who banks carbon. With the decline in pollution-intensive manufacturing in Western Europe and North America, public pressure on banks that finance such industries in developing countries is likely to rise.' (Wright, 2006).

In the insurance world, AIG recently announced it would 'dedicate resources to the development of market-based solutions that address climate change.' And Reinsurance giant Swiss Re has already developed the world's first insurance product for CDM transaction risk for RNK Capital, insuring against the uncertainty of project registration under the Kyoto Protocol. According to Ben Lashkari, head of emissions at Swiss Re's Environmental and Commodity Markets, 'The policy provides liquidity, it provides confidence, and it basically makes the carbon market more of a mature, functioning market.' (Hall, 2006). While currently directed at the compliance carbon market, new insurance products like those pioneered by Swiss Re may be a harbinger of things to come for the voluntary carbon market.

In general, corporations cite five reasons for participating in the voluntary market:

- Experience and clout as a way to influence future regulatory requirements and policy setting
- Preparation for potential regulatory requirements
- Competitive differentiation as consumers become increasingly concerned about climate change, including being able to offer products that are 'carbon neutral' (perhaps for price premiums that generate a net profit for the companies retailing the products in question)
- Inclusion in company-wide corporate social responsibility or sustainability strategies
- Better access to capital by helping attract investment and secure project finance
- Ability to recruit, retain, and reward staff because of 'good actor' perception

Public sector institutions

Governments at the local, regional and federal level have all emerged as voluntary buyers of carbon credits. For example, the cities of Chicago,

Oakland, Berkeley, Portland, and Aspen in the US have joined the Chicago Climate Exchange. In Australia, the states of New South Wales and Victoria have both said they will invest in offset projects in order to offset their emissions. And the UK government recently announced it would buy carbon credits in order to take all of its operations carbon neutral.

What's driving these decisions? Public sector institutions probably have two main reasons for entering the voluntary carbon market as buyers: (1) they are interested in advancing the market as a means of attracting private sector capital toward costly environmental problems; and (2) they sense their constituency's desire for action on climate change and so want to be seen as leading by example. Of these, the latter is probably the most important.

Social sector institutions

Non-profit institutional buyers are driven by the importance of 'walking the talk,' public relations, and philanthropic aims that range from ecological restoration to sustainable development. There are a number of environmental organizations that believe markets provide a promising new approach to conservation finance. There are also a number of corporate foundations, universities and political organizations – both national and international – that have taken it upon themselves to seed the voluntary carbon market by stepping in as buyers of carbon credits. The key driver of demand among these buyers, then, is the degree to which they believe the market can drive environmental and social benefits.

Market trends

Some investors think that, as regulation comes online in the US and more sectors are included in the EU ETS, voluntary carbon credits will see a jump in value not unlike that experienced by CDM credits once the Kyoto Protocol went into effect.

To wit, Climate Wedge Ltd. started the world's first voluntary carbon offset fund in July 2005. The Cheyne Climate Wedge Fund invests in high-quality offsets for carbon dioxide emissions for large-scale corporate and institutional buyers. 'Our view of the world is that the use of voluntary carbon offsets is going to grow dramatically,' says Michael Molitor, the Fund's CEO. His reasoning: it's the only thing we can do to slow down the growth in emissions over the next two decades (Walker, 2006).

For the most part the drivers of the voluntary carbon market look set to grow in the coming years, but it should be remembered that the market is far from mainstream at this point and uncertainty abounds. Fortunately, registries, standards and exchanges are evolving to help streamline the voluntary carbon market and consolidate market information as potential buyers push for increased transparency. It should become easier, then, for buyers and sellers to grasp both the risks and the opportunities associated with this dynamic market in the coming years.

References

Anderson, C. (2006) 'California At the Forefront', *The Ecosystem Marketplace,* www.ecosystemmarketplace.com/

Arnold, T. Interviewed by: Amanda Hawn, July 2006

Biello, D. (2005) 'Climate friendly fuels', *The Ecosystem Marketplace,* www.ecosystemmarketplace.com/

Bank of New York Company (2006) 'The Bank of New York creates global registrar and custody service for voluntary carbon units', *Business Wire Inc.*

Butzengeiger, S. (2005) 'Voluntary compensation of GHG emissions: selection criteria and implications for the international climate policy system', *Report No. 1 by The HWWI Research Programme International Climate Policy,* Hamburg Institute of International Economics, Hamburg

Capoor, K. and Ambrosi, P. (2006) *State and Trends of the Carbon Market 2006,* The World Bank, Washington DC

Clarke, D. (2003) 'Scaling Down Carbon Finance', *Environmental Finance,* London, Fulton Publishing

Davidsen, A. (2006) Presentation at GreenT Forum: Raising the Bar for Voluntary Environmental Credit Markets, New York. New York, 2–3 May, 2006

Grobbel, C., Maly, J. and Molitor, M. (2004) 'Preparing for a low-carbon future' *McKinsey Quarterly,* McKinsey and Company

Hall, J. (2006) 'Climate Change: For Insurers, The Best Defense May Be a Good Offense', *The Ecosystem Marketplace,* www.ecosystemmarketplace.com/

Hamilton, K. (2006) 'Navigating a Nebula: Institutional Use of the U.S. Voluntary Carbon Market,' Masters Thesis at the Yale School of Forestry and Environmental Studies

Hawn, A. (2005) 'eBay Shoppers and Subsistence Farmers Meet on Virtual Ground', *The Ecosystem Marketplace,* www.ecosystemmarketplace.com/

HSBC (2005) 'HSBC carbon neutral pilot project,' downloaded from HSBC website

Janson-Smith, T. Interviewed by: Katherine Hamilton July 2006

Kvale, L. Interviewed by: Walker Wright July 2006

Molitor, M. (2005) 'Carbon Volunteers', *Carbon Finance,* London, Fulton Publishing

Murray, M. E. and Petersen, J. E. (2004) 'Payback and Currencies of Energy, Carbon Dioxide and Money for a 60kW Photovoltaic Array', Technical Report, Oberlin College, Oberlin, Ohio

Neil, Dan (2005) 'TerraPass eases drivers' minds', *Los Angeles Times* Feb. 2, 2005

New Forests Advisory Pty Ltd (2005) '2005 Global Retail Carbon Market Report', Prepared for The Ecosystem Marketplace

Rau, A. Interviewed by: Amanda Hawn June 2006

Sampson, N. (2006) 'Issue Paper on Inclusion of Terrestrial Carbon Sequestration Activities in Voluntary GHG Registries and Market Trading programmes', *EPA Task 4 Working Draft*

Seely, R. (2006) Presentation at GreenT Forum: Raising the Bar for Voluntary Environmental Credit Markets, New York. New York, 2–3 May, 2006

Taiyab, N. (2006) 'Exploring the Market for Voluntary Carbon Offsets', *International Institute for Environment and Development*

The Climate Group (2005) 'Carbon Down Profits Up 2nd Edition', *Environmental Finance,* London, Fulton Publishing, pp26–27

Trexler, M., Broekhoff, D. J., and Kosloff, L. H. (2006) 'A Statistically Driven Approach to Offset Based GHG Additionality Determinations: What Can We

Learn', *Sustainable Development Law and Policy,* vol. VI, issue 2, American University Washington College of Law, Washington DC
Trexler, M. Interviewed by Katherine Hamilton May 2006
Walker, C. (2006) 'The Voluntary Carbon Markets Difference Maker: Michael Molitor', *The Ecosystem Marketplace,* www.ecosystemmarketplace.com/
Wright, C. (2006) 'Carbon Neutrality Draws Praise, Raises Expectations for HSBC', *The Ecosystem Marketplace,* www.ecosystemmarketplace.com/
Zwick, S. (2006) 'Green Goal: Soccer Enters the Carbon Markets', *The Ecosystem Marketplace,* www.ecosystemmarketplace.com/

Websites

Globe Scan/BBC 'Current Energy Use Seen to Threaten Environment, Economy, Peace', www.mypublicopinion.org/ July 2006
The Clean Development Website, www.cdm.unfccc.int/
'GHG Protocol Initiative: For Project Accounting', *World Business Council for Sustainable Development and World Resources Institute,* www.ghgprotocol.org/
'Voluntary Reporting of Greenhouse Gases', *Energy Information Administration Website,* www.eia.doe.gov/oiaf/1605/2ndbroc.html

3

How Does the Voluntary Carbon Market Relate to the US REC Market?

Walker L. Wright

Ask Tom Arnold, chief environmental officer of carbon offsets retailer TerraPass, why his company likes supporting new renewable energy projects in addition to projects that just avoid emitting greenhouse gases at pre-existing facilities, and he'll tell you the answer is fairly simple: 'A big part of our job is explaining offsets to consumers,' says Arnold. 'Telling people that they have an opportunity to do good is a much more powerful message than telling them they have a chance to do less bad . . . Sit in a room teaching eight people about how carbon offsets work and you can see when they get it,' he continues. 'People get the iconic image of a wind turbine' (Arnold, 2006).

Driven by the purchasing preferences of its customers, TerraPass sells verified GHG emission reductions not only from industrial efficiency projects, but also from biomass energy and wind energy projects. The company acquires offsets from biomass energy and industrial efficiency projects on the Chicago Climate Exchange, but for offsets from wind energy projects, it turns to the established US market for renewable energy certificates (RECs).

In conducting research on the voluntary carbon market, one cannot help but bump into the market for RECs, Renewable Obligation Certificates (ROCs), Tradable Renewable Certificates (TRCs), Green Tags and Green Energy Certificates, as they are variously known. To wit, Arnold says TerraPass was struggling to find a third party verifier for the GHG emission reduction projects in its portfolio when the company stumbled upon the REC market. 'People in the carbon world (who now have offices) were still working at their kitchen tables at that point,' remembers Arnold. 'All of a sudden we realized there was this REC world that looked a little bit more mature' (Arnold, 2006).

Arnold soon struck up a partnership with the largest verifier of RECs in North America, and TerraPass now advertises that, '33 per cent of your TerraPass purchase consists of Green-e certified renewable energy'.

Some find this blurring of the line between the voluntary carbon market and the REC market exciting since it suggests potential synergies between the two markets and could expand sources of supply and demand for both of them. Others, however, fear that the markets are fundamentally different and might ultimately undermine one another if policy makers and market participants fail to appreciate these differences. Before we delve into this debate more deeply, however, let's review what RECs are and how they are traded.

What are RECs?

Flowing along wires via power transmission and distribution systems that make up the electrical grid, electricity makes its way to where it is needed to provide light, heat and mechanical energy on all sides of the globe. The electricity humanity consumes employs power from a compilation of sources. Currently, around 80 per cent of the world's consumed electricity derives from fossil fuels[1] – traditional sources that harm human health, degrade ecosystems and add to global warming. According to the US Environmental Protection Agency, production of electricity from fossil fuels causes more air pollution than any other source.

Recognition of the need to decrease the amount of electricity derived from fossil fuels has increased interest in renewable energy products – which harness wind, sunlight, plant matter or heat from the earth's core – to produce electricity that is environmentally friendly. In turn, this interest has led governments and international organizations to mandate the incorporation of more renewable power sources into grids around the world. According to a report released by the Renewable Energy Policy Network for the 21st Century (REN21), at least 48 countries already have some kind of renewable energy promotion policy in place, including China and India (Wright, 2006).

RECs are one of the more interesting mechanisms that have emerged to incentivise the production of renewable energy in Europe, Australia and the US. In the US, RECs represent the environmental attributes of a unit, typically one MWh of electricity generated from renewable fuels. The renewable attributes of that electricity are then sold separately as a REC; one REC may be issued for each unit of renewable electricity produced. In other words, programmes have been established that separate renewable electricity generation into two commodities:

1 RECs representing the green attributes, or social and environmental benefits, of generation renewable sources.
2 Energy produced by a renewable generator delivered to the grid, where it blends with electricity from regular generators in a generic 'soup' of electrons following the path of least resistance (Gewin, 2005).

There is no one distinct market for RECs but rather a potpourri of fragmented markets in which prices and circumstances vary. Unlike the voluntary market for RECs in Europe and Australia, which has been kept separate from the voluntary carbon market, the REC market in the US has begun to converge with that for carbon offsets. For this reason, the following discussion focuses on the REC market in the US.

The compliance market

Like the global carbon market, the US REC market features both compliance and voluntary segments. We will turn first to the compliance side of the market.

In the absence of federal regulation, many states have used Renewable Portfolio Standards (RPS) to provide incentives for renewable energy. RPS programmes require electric utilities to use renewable energy sources to provide some percentage of the electricity they sell to consumers each year.

Utilities may meet RPS requirements in any of three ways: they may build renewable energy sources themselves, they may buy green power from projects connected to the grid or they may purchase RECs from renewable energy providers. In general, regulated utilities employ all three of these strategies, but it is worth noting that RECs – because they are not bound to the same geographic or physical constraints as commodity electricity – represent the most flexible mechanism for compliance.

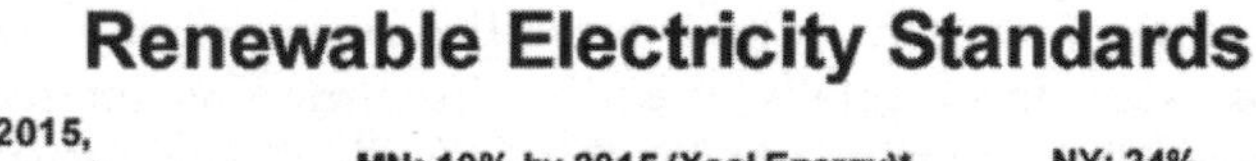

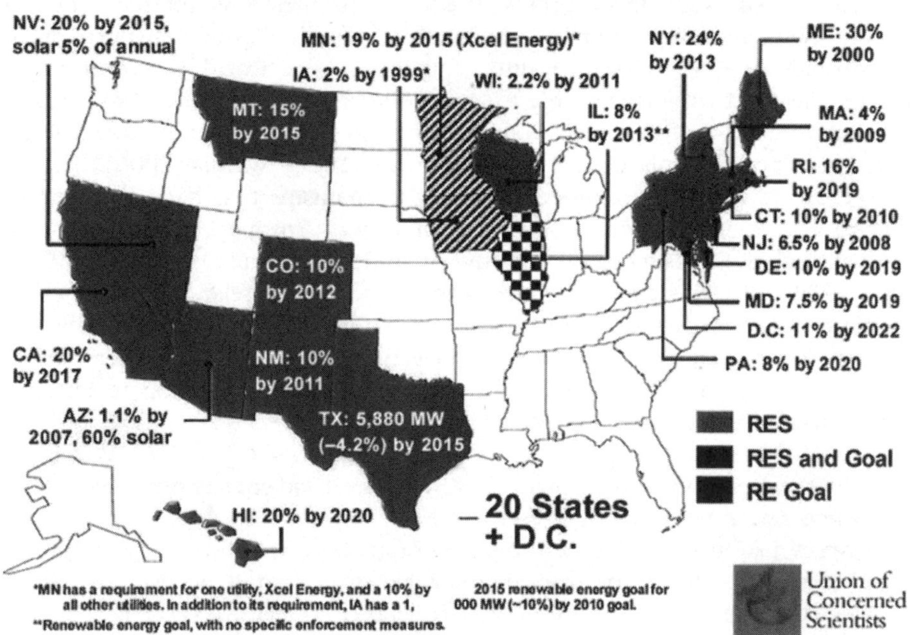

Figure 3.1 *A map of the RPS standards in the US*

Note: In the US, state governments continually update RPS standards.

Collectively, states with strong RPS schemes have the potential to create significant demand for RECs, particularly in future years as renewable energy targets increase and policies take effect. Although REC trading has not yet taken off in most states, market observers estimate that nearly 8,000,000MWh of RECs were used for RPS compliance in New England and Texas in 2004, where REC tracking systems are in place. Given current REC trading prices and market estimates, compliance REC markets are believed to be worth more than US$100 million annually. By 2010, forecasts show RPS policies will require more than 45,000,000MWh of RECs or renewable energy generation (Holt and Bird, 2005, pp26–27). In fact the market has the potential to be much larger if states such as California approve the use of RECs for RPS compliance.

Prices of RECs used for RPS compliance are affected by available supplies, the quality of the renewable energy resources in the region, the ability to site new projects, rules regarding geographic eligibility and banking, and the level of the noncompliance penalty (which essentially sets a cap on REC prices). For instance, recent prices have ranged from as low as US$0.70MWh for existing renewables in Maine and Connecticut to a more common US$10.00–15.00/MWh in Texas, and as high as US$35.00–49.00/MWh for new renewable energy sources in New England. Solar specific renewable energy certificates (S-RECs) in New Jersey fluctuated between US$115.00 and 265.00/MWh in March 2006. Historically, REC prices have been highest in New England, where supply is constrained by banking and trading rules that limit market liquidity and by the fact that incentive and rebate programmes lag behind other regions in encouraging the financing of renewable energy projects. Within any given trading area, market prices generally differ by resource type, vintage and volume. In January 2005, Holt and Bird estimated that total value of the compliance market could reach US$608 million by 2010.

The voluntary market

As in the carbon market, the voluntary market for RECs is more fragmented than the compliance market, with a variety of businesses offering a wide array of products. The flexibility of voluntary RECs allows the consumer to support renewable energy development through certificate purchases regardless of access to green power products through retail power providers and without having to switch to an alternative electricity provider.

Numerous companies now offer certificate-based green power products, and many now allow individuals and businesses to buy RECs online.[2] In general, voluntary RECs are sold to consumers in one of three ways:

1. they are retailed as a stand-alone product, either regionally or nationally;
2. they are bundled with energy derived from traditional sources to produce green energy products;
3. they are sold through a contract promising a future stream of RECs from new or planned renewable energy installations.

Stand-alone products (unbundled)

A growing number of marketers sell unbundled RECs to commercial and individual users who are anxious to support the development of renewable energy projects.

In January 2005 the National Renewable Energy Laboratory (NREL) estimated that more than 650,000MWh of stand-alone RECs were sold through 20 companies to about 5000 retail customers in 2003. In October 2005 another NREL report concluded that retail sales of RECs sold separately from electricity, grew nearly threefold, reaching 1.7,000,000MWh in 2004 (Bird and Swezey, 2005, pp11; Holt and Bird, 2005, pp28).

For the most part stand-alone RECs are marketed to non-residential and commercial consumers such as businesses, universities and government agencies. Recently, sales in this niche market have grown considerably. Green-e (see 'Certify it'), the leading REC verifier in the US, has reported noteworthy increments in growth for retail sales of Green-e certified stand-alone RECs since 2002. Recent data indicate that Green-e certifies over half of the REC market (Holt and Bird, 2005, pp28).

Since commercial consumers often want to support local programmes for branding purposes and reasons of corporate social responsibility, companies

Table 3.1 *REC sales in voluntary markets*

Year	MWh	Retail consumers	Portion of all voluntary green power sales (%)	RECs as % of retail green power purchases
2003	650,000	5000	17	1.20

Source: Holt and Bird, 2005

Table 3.2 *Certified REC customers and sales for leading voluntary certifier Green-e*

	Customers				Sales (MWh)			
	2002	2003	2004	2005[a]	2002	2003	2004	2005[b]
Residential	2000	2700	2100	2400	8000	8000	7000	10,000
Non-residential	200	400	500	800	68,000	332,000	756,000	1,500,000
Retail total	2200	3100	2600	3200	76,000	340,000	763,000	1,510,000
Wholesale[c]	20	50	70	100	73,000	1,494,000	2,058,000	2,890,000
Total	2200	3200	2700	3300	150,000	1,835,000	2,821,000	4,400,000

Notes:

a These are preliminary numbers for Green-e certified sales in 2005. The final numbers will be available from Green-e in the annual verification report to be published in October 2006.

b Ibid.

c A portion (10–20 per cent) of the RECs transacted on the wholesale level are used to supply Green-e certified products selling RECs on the retail market.

Source: Center for Resource Solutions and Kvale (August 2006); Holt and Bird, 2005

retailing RECs often focus on a defined geographic area. Pennsylvania-based Community Energy Inc. (CEI), for example, markets RECs from new wind energy projects in Pennsylvania, New York and West Virginia to end-use customers in these and other north-east states.[3] The Bonneville Environmental Foundation (BEF), a non-profit organization based in Portland, Oregon, pursues a similar sales model in the Pacific Northwest, where it sells Green Tags generated by new wind, solar and biomass projects in Oregon, Washington and Wyoming to businesses, government agencies and other large energy consumers in the area.

Other retailers ignore geographic boundaries when sourcing RECs for on-sale as a stand-alone product. Taking advantage of the fact that RECs are fungible across state lines, retailers such as Georgia-based Sterling Planet choose to market RECs sourced from renewable energy generators located throughout the nation.

Bundled products

The second main type of transaction in the voluntary market is the sale of green energy products (with RECs embedded in them) to consumers who are willing to pay price premiums associated with the development of renewable energy sources. When RECs are bundled with electricity and sold as green power, clean power or renewable electricity, it is worth noting that the use of RECs is often invisible to the consumer. Rather, energy retailers act on behalf of the consumer, purchasing wholesale and retiring RECs in order to substantiate their claims to the provision of green energy. In 2005 NREL estimated that in 2003, utilities collectively purchased roughly 420,000MWh of RECs to supply green pricing programmes, accounting for 33 per cent of total retail sales.

Companies that are not utilities also commonly purchase RECs at wholesale to provide bundled renewable energy products in competitive power markets. This means purchasing RECs within region and bundling them with electricity from the power pool. NREL estimates that almost 2,700,000MWh of renewable energy from existing and new sources was sold to retail customers in competitive markets in 2004, up from 1,900,000MWh in 2003 (Bird and Swezey, 2005, pp 11).

Table 3.3 *Utility use of RECs to supply green pricing programs*

	Utility purchases of RECs for green pricing programs (MWh)	***% of total sales***
2002	103,000	11%
2003	419,000	33%

Source: Holt and Bird 2005

For example, Green Mountain Energy – the largest retail provider of green energy to residential and commercial customers in the US – purchases RECs through wholesale transactions on the voluntary market and then bundles them with commodity electricity in order to supply green energy to customers in states such as New Jersey, Pennsylvania, Ohio, and Texas. Green Mountain claims its power product is 100 per cent renewable and pollution free, generated by 50 per cent regional wind and 50 per cent regional small hydro. In this scenario, when a customer purchases the renewable product, Green Mountain matches the monthly electricity usage with clean energy generated from renewable sources, while the local utility continues to provide service and maintenance. By paying an extra US¢90 (less than a penny) per kWh on top of local utility charges, a typical New Jersey household using 750kWh per month is said to avoid contributing 2.04 metric tons (4,500lbs) of carbon dioxide into the air over the course of a year.[4]

Forward selling of RECs

Selling a future stream of RECs from new or planned renewable energy projects is the third approach retailers may take when marketing RECs on the voluntary market. Vermont-based Native Energy employs this business model through its Windbuilders product, which helped support the development of the 750kW Rosebud Sioux wind turbine in South Dakota. Native Energy sells RECs across the 25-year expected life of the turbine, discounting prices to account for the time value of money and the risk of non-delivery. Because Native Energy markets RECs from prospective projects, the company agrees to support an alternate project or purchase RECs from other new renewable facilities if the initial project is not completed.

Generally, project developers support the forward selling of RECs because it helps them finance up-front project costs. Forward selling, however, has been limited in scope to date because of the risks associated with the potential for non-delivery.

Certify it

Ensuring that the promised social and environmental benefits are delivered is not just a concern for those interested in the forward selling of RECs. Rather the issue is germane to the REC market as a whole and lies at the heart of conversations about verification and certification.

The two largest verifiers and certifiers of RECs for the voluntary market in the US are the Center for Resource Solutions and the Environmental Resources Trust. The non-profit Center for Resource Solutions established the Green-e Renewable Electricity Program in 1997 to build consumer confidence in green power during the electricity restructuring process of the mid 1990s. The nation's first voluntary verification and certification programme for renewable electricity products, Green-e sets environmental product standards and requires companies to disclose information about their products.[5] Green marketers who wish to transact Green-e certified products pay an annual fee and agree to an annual audit of their marketing claims and transactions. In return, the marketers profit from consumer confidence in their products.

The Green-e TRC Standard is the most widely used in the US, with more than 30 different products offering Green-e certified RECs. The total sales of these products exceeded 4 million Green-e certified RECs in 2005.[6] In order to earn Green-e certification, a renewable energy product must derive at least 25 per cent of its electricity supply from approved renewable sources. If a portion of the electricity is non-renewable, the air emissions must be equal to or lower than those produced by conventional electricity. All RECs used in Green-e certified REC products have to be from new renewable facilities. Additionally, the renewable energy used cannot come from a facility that has been mandated by a government agency or produced in order to satisfy a government RPS.[7] All Green-e certified products undergo annual audits on power generation and marketing claims.

The Environmental Resources Trust (ERT) defines a REC slightly differently than the Center for Resource Solutions. ERT holds that RECs are simply a record of the claim of energy generation placed into the grid. In order to verify this claim ERT will check the specific environmental attributes included in the REC in question and, if desired, will calculate the specific emissions savings resulting from the power they helped introduce to the grid. In addition, ERT will conduct a post-sale audit to verify that RECs have not been sold or 'counted' more than once.

The Environmental Resources Trust's EcoPower SM programme both certifies renewable electricity to meet certain environmental standards and works with suppliers to provide the requested renewable electricity mix to corporations and municipalities. ERT's EcoPower SM label thus sees itself as different from the Green-e programme in the following way: 'ERT works to develop a clean power product tailored to the organization's needs in addition to its certification role while Green-e acts purely as a certifying 'stamp' for various clean power products.'[8]

Whichever verification methodology and certification label retailers choose to use, most will tell you that third-party verification of a project's RECs has become increasingly important in recent years. And if the voluntary market for RECs is to continue growing, all agree that transparency and careful project accounting are necessary to maintain consumer confidence in such an intangible product.

Market trends

Despite its recent growth, the voluntary REC market is much smaller than the compliance market and prices are generally lower. Estimating the value of the voluntary market is more complicated than for compliance markets, given the variety of products offered, differences in the price of products sold to residential and non-residential consumers, and the variety of resources used to supply the market.

In order to arrive at a rough indication of the value of this market, NREL applies a range of US$5/MWh to US$15/MWh, based on current retail prices and recognizing that sales to large non-residential customers dominate retail sales. NREL market observers suggest the voluntary market for RECs is currently worth US$15 million to US$45 million annually, but think it could grow in value to as much as US$300 million annually by 2010. Under a low-growth scenario, then, the market might support 8,000,000MWh annually in 2010. High-growth scenarios, meanwhile, predict the market will soon support 61,000,000MWh annually (Holt and Bird, 2005, pp36).

On an individual basis, REC certificates often sell for a premium of US$0.015–$0.04 per kWh, but there are large price spreads. For example, while 3 Phases Energy Services and BEF sell mostly wind generated RECs at a premium of US$0.02 per kWh, Mainstay Energy sells one REC product, '100 per cent Fossil Free Solar' for US$0.20 per kWh.

RECs and the voluntary carbon market

As prices rise and fall in the REC market, one of the most interesting market trends is the increasing convergence of the voluntary markets for RECs and carbon offsets. In particular, when retail prices for RECs drop below retail prices for carbon, suppliers and brokers are anxious to sell RECs into the carbon market.

Look closely at many of the contracts for RECs on the U.S. voluntary market, and you will find they mention the GHG emissions that will be avoided as a result of the project generating the REC. In these cases, the demand for RECs could be construed as a latent demand for carbon emission reductions. Alternatively, the demand for emission reductions may really be driven by the demand for a more diversified energy base. Either way, buyers in the US increasingly are looking to both the REC and carbon markets to advance action on the intertwined issues of energy policy and climate change. As these buyers – and the retailers who respond to them – drive the carbon market and REC market toward one another, two important questions arise. First, are the respective verification and tracking systems of the two markets compatible? And second, what happens to the REC market if a robust regulated carbon market comes onto the scene in the US?

RECs are generally converted to carbon offsets by finding the amount of CO_2 emitted by local fossil-fuel-burning power plants per kWh. For example, to calculate greenhouse gas offsets for a wind turbine Native Energy will be building, verifiers gathered information from emissions data for the local power control area and found that the local power plants generate 2.370lbs of CO_2 for every kWh of energy they generate. Native Energy then discounted this rate to account for the probability that power plants will reduce this ratio (emissions/kWh) in the future through technology upgrades. The final conversion factor, then, was found to be 0.0014lbs of CO_2 reduced per kWh over a 25-year period (Hamilton, 2006, pp29).

Those who support the idea of selling RECs as a form of carbon offset hope that tracking systems might soon help marry the REC market with the carbon market through an elegant form of electronic banking. Under such a system, RECs would be issued with a unique serial number that could be transferred from a renewable energy tracking system onto a set of carbon registry books if a buyer wanted to use them for carbon benefits (Gewin, 2005).

In fact, CRS is currently creating a certification standard for retail greenhouse gas products that use RECs and other GHG reductions from approved third party verification standards.[9] CRS' steps toward certification of RECs for retail greenhouse gas products under its Green-e programme are driven by the fact that numerous retailers in the US are already offering Green-e certified RECs as carbon offsets to institutions and individuals (e.g. Terrapass, The Carbon Fund). Lars Kvale of CRS says the goal of the retail GHG product standard is, 'to make sure things match up at the back end and to protect buyers from issues such as double counting.'[10]

Others believe that even with a newly designed and carefully crafted tracking system, cross-market transactions are inappropriate since the verification processes for RECs and carbon credits are innately different. 'This market crossover can be a problem primarily because RECs, in marked contrast to carbon offsets, have no additionality requirement,' argues Mark Trexler, president of Trexler Climate + Energy services. 'Selling "non-additional" RECs into the carbon offset market undercuts the additionality requirement that is at the heart of carbon offsets, and could devalue the voluntary carbon offset market.'

Just as some carbon market participants fear the expansion of the voluntary REC market could undermine the voluntary carbon market's ability to drive real benefits, some participants in the REC market fear the future expansion of carbon markets in the US could impinge upon the ability of the REC market to contribute to GHG emission reductions. If emission allowances in a regulated cap-and-trade scheme are granted exclusively to existing emitters (i.e. utilities) rather than renewable energy facilities, then any emission reductions at utilities will simply allow them to use fewer allowances. And since these allowances have value in a cap-and-trade system, any allowances that are not used on-site will be traded for use off-site. The result, then, is that the renewable energy project that has been financed, in part, by RECs has succeeded in adding more electricity to the grid, but has failed to reduce emissions on a system-wide scale. 'Under a cap-and-trade system, the only way to reduce air pollution for the associated pollutant is to reduce the number of allowances,' explains Rob Harmon of the Bonneville Environmental Foundation. 'Without the ability to claim air quality improvements, the demand for new renewable energy will likely be substantially reduced.'

On balance

Clearly, the evolving carbon and REC markets in the US have both important similarities and important differences. In general, people on all sides of the debate over whether or not RECs should be sold as carbon offsets agree that close attention to the verification and registration of renewable energy projects will grow ever more important in the days, months and years ahead. If the two markets are to co-exist peacefully, policy-makers in the REC and carbon markets must stay in conversation with one another. Fortunately, it seems, this dialogue has already begun.

What the experts think

In order to get a better sense of the arguments for and against crossover between the REC and carbon markets in the US, we have asked two experts to take opposite sides of the debate. In the following section, Mark Trexler, president of Trexler Climate + Energy Services, will explain the case against trading RECs into the carbon market. Rob Harmon, vice president of renewable energy programmes at the Bonneville Environmental Foundation, will then describe why he thinks the convergence of the two markets is a good thing, since products have already been developed to address many of the important issues concerning additionality.

In a second editorial, Harmon will then discuss why he thinks the REC market must be factored into any future market-based approach toward carbon regulation in the US.

Renewable Energy Certificates to carbon offsets: What's the right exchange rate?

Mark Trexler

A slightly different version of this article first appeared on the ClimateBiz website, see www.climatebiz.org

The conversion of RECs to carbon offsets is increasingly common. Many of the websites offering to render consumers carbon neutral are actually doing so by purchasing and retiring RECs. How should we feel about that?

One can make the case that RECs and offsets should be exchanged in different markets. RECs basically are simply MWh of electricity produced from a qualifying renewable energy technology of a qualifying vintage. In voluntary markets, people buy RECs because they want to help promote renewable energy. The REC may not even include the environmental attributes of that MWh, which some people strip off and sell separately – although I've always had trouble understanding what you're really buying through a REC if its environmental attributes have been stripped out. Even when environmental attributes are included, you should have realistic expectations as to what you're getting. Is the quantification of CO_2 displacement, for example, based on actual system modelling, on the average system mix, or on some other measure? And to the extent that the environmental benefits are indirect (since they occur at the utility where generation is displaced rather than at the point of production), you have to accept that you probably don't have any ownership rights to those displaced emissions and that they're subject to double counting (since the utility will effectively be counting the same reduction, whether intentionally or not).

A carbon offset is conceptually different. It represents an action that prevents the emission (or causes the sequestration) of 1tCO_2e, (reflecting the existence of several key greenhouse gases and the use of CO_2e as a common metric). In voluntary markets, people buy carbon offsets because they want to reduce their global warming footprint. Thus, the carbon offset is the environmental benefit associated with the activity being undertaken. But this can't be directly measured; instead, you have to make assumptions about a carbon offset project's 'baseline,' and what CO_2e emissions would have been without the project. Often, the most complicated part of generating a carbon offset is demonstrating the additionality of the activity being undertaken. Additionality refers to whether the activity in question is or is not business as usual, that is, is it happening as a result of the commodity value of the carbon offsets, or would it have happened even without carbon offsets having a value? This question is key to answering the question of whether a project actually results in emissions reductions from the baseline.

With RECs, the commodity is a physical and measurable unit (electricity) and the environmental attributes come along for the ride. There's nothing complicated about generating a REC if you have the right technology. In carbon offsets, the commodity is a construct based on divergence from an assumed baseline. It can be very complicated to generate a carbon offset in cases where the baseline is difficult to pin down.

As long as the two commodities are kept separate they can peacefully co-exist, some buyers purchasing RECs to promote renewable energy, other buyers purchasing carbon offsets to reduce their global warming footprint. Things get interesting when people try to find ways to cross from one market into the other. This is a relatively new phenomenon, as REC prices have fallen dramatically in much of the US. Several years ago, many RECs sold for $20–30/MWh electricity (the equivalent of $20–30/ton of CO_2e); carbon offsets were selling at $5–10/ton. So it didn't make sense to try to convert RECs into carbon offsets. If you had a choice as to whether to generate RECs or carbon offsets from a project, you would choose RECs.

Today, REC prices can be as low as $1–2/MWh. REC brokers are happy to try and sell those RECs as carbon offsets at $5–10/ton. Indeed, retail carbon offset providers are selling RECs along with, or instead of more conventional carbon offsets like landfill gas or coalmine methane recovery.

This market crossover can be a problem primarily because RECs, in marked contrast to carbon offsets, have no additionality requirement. Thus, RECs may not reflect the same incremental environmental benefit generally required of carbon offsets. In the US, for example, wind farms produce more than 20,000,000MWh of electricity per year, dwarfing the size of the REC market. So even if the REC market intends to increase the demand for renewable energy over time, we can supply a lot of RECs from renewables that can realistically be thought of as business as usual. Selling non-additional RECs into the carbon offset market undercuts the additionality requirement that is at the heart of carbon offsets, and could devalue the voluntary carbon offset market.

Lower REC and carbon offset prices might seem desirable for purchasers. But if lower prices reflect the absence of environmental benefit, it's a high price to pay. That's a good reason to keep the two commodities separate until and unless they can be put on a level additionality playing field. That would involve quite a different approach than is current reflected in the generation of RECs.

Renewable Energy Certificates and carbon offsets: What informed customers need to know

Robert Harmon

There is much discussion in this book about how RECs should or should not interact with the GHG market. As a matter of full disclosure, the Bonneville Environmental Foundation (BEF) has offered customers the option to reduce their CO_2 footprint through the purchase of Green Tags (RECs) since 2000. BEF launched the first Internet-based CO_2 calculator in 2001, after meticulous analysis with the Northwest Power and Conservation Council and then with the Climate Neutral Network, which endorsed our methodology.

It should be noted at the start that BEF, along with all other voluntary REC marketers of which we are aware, believes that the voluntary REC market must work alongside of, and in addition to, the compliance markets, to ensure that both markets prosper and create demand for additional renewable energy development. With that understanding, what do we know about the voluntary REC market?

The most recent data from the National Renewable Energy Laboratory show that more than half a million customers purchased more than 6.200,000kWh of renewable energy in the voluntary market in 2004; a year the market grew 62 per cent. To provide some context, if all of that were generated from wind (which it was not) it would equal over 2,000MW of installed wind energy capacity. The voluntary REC market is perhaps the largest voluntary market of environmental certificates/credits of any kind.

What do all these voluntary REC customers want? Some critics of RECs as GHG offsets have argued that customers purchase RECs simply to help promote renewable energy, with little concern for GHG emissions. This is simply not the case. As the article that follows this one (Clearing the Air) demonstrates, the primary driver of the voluntary REC market is GHG emissions reductions. In press release after press release CO_2 reduction is cited as the primary driver. RECs are a cost-effective, easily understood method of getting to the heart of the CO_2 problem by changing the mix of electricity away from fossil fuels and toward renewable energy. Customers understand this and want to participate.

There is consensus that the presence of renewable energy systems on the grid reduces CO_2. Some REC marketers calculate the CO_2 offset based on the displacement of average emissions for the regional electric grid; some choose to analyse what resources are likely not to be built as new renewable energy comes on line; and some choose to look carefully at the effect on 'spinning reserves' – those resources that 'stand by' as electricity demand and supply fluctuate up and down during the day. Space limitations prevent me from going into depth regarding which option might be preferred, but it is clear that CO_2 reductions do indeed happen when renewable energy facilities operate. Over the next year, I anticipate that a consensus will be built around a common methodology. This is all good news.

Whether the emissions reductions renewable energy systems create are delivered to the customer is another matter. In the US there is currently no cap-and-trade (or any other) regulation in place for CO_2. Because the government has not asserted a right of ownership or otherwise modified the CO_2 property right, the RECs and any associated emissions reductions therein belong first to the party owning the renewable generating facility, and then to any party to whom they sell the REC. Government policy may assign ownership in the future, and that issue is addressed in the paper below (Clearing the Air). At this time, customers who buy quality REC products certified by Green-e can be assured that the CO_2 emissions benefits are being sold to them, and only to them. That is more good news.

Customers also want to know that their purchases create benefits above and beyond what would happen without their purchase. Some refer to this concept as additionality. To address the vital consumer and environmental protection issues associated with selling RECs, a diverse group of stakeholders formed Green-e in 1997. This stakeholder group created national standards that address the vast majority of concerns regarding additionality, and create a marketplace in which customers can purchase with confidence. For instance, under Green-e rules:

- only renewable energy facilities that were built after 1 January, 1997 qualify to sell RECs;
- no RECs that are sold into mandatory markets can be sold into voluntary markets;
- transactions are audited to ensure no double counting;
- all marketing materials are reviewed to ensure accuracy;
- carbon claim methodologies must be clearly documented.

These rules have allowed the market to thrive. Critics who argue that RECs may not contain environmental benefits; that those benefits can be double counted; or that GHG reduction methodologies for RECs do not exist, misunderstand the rules put in place by Green-e or simply lack awareness that Green-e is the premier quality standard for voluntary offset purchases from RECs in the US.

Concerns have also been raised regarding a massive oversupply of RECs. This concern is misguided. RECs from facilities that were built prior to 1997 don't qualify under Green-e, and the vast majority of RECs currently being generated are assigned to compliance markets and are hence disqualified from Green-e certified products. As I write this article, a well-respected REC broker tells me that the US REC market is 'overbid'. That could of course change tomorrow, or next week, or next year. Just six months ago there were significant numbers of RECs looking for customers. Such is the reality of markets. REC prices vary by region, as a function of supply and demand.

Green-e rules have addressed the vast majority of concerns regarding additionality. However, some still argue that projects should have to demonstrate a financial need in order to qualify for voluntary GHG payments.

Creating a financial yardstick to determine if a project is additional is essentially impossible. Not only would it be excruciatingly time consuming to examine the financial statements for each project, but there is no guarantee that the data presented would be accurate at the time it was presented, or that it would represent the final costs of the project. Who would decide what the 'proper' amount of profit would be? What costs would be allowed or disallowed? What if a project developer chose to use union labor and that raised costs (and potentially quality)? Would that be approved? A financial yardstick creates an incentive to artificially raise the cost of a generating facility to prove the need for additional funds.

A final suggestion from critics is that a renewable energy facility must be built after GHG or REC payments are received in order to prove additionality.

There is no reason to believe that gathering voluntary GHG payment for a project prior to its construction is any more or less likely to guarantee its additionality than paying for the project costs over several years. Gathering the payments up front is simply a different financing mechanism. Most REC marketers choose to ask the renewable energy generator to take the financing risk, and the result of this model has been the addition of thousands of MW of new renewable generation. The number of new MW installed under the collect-the-premiums-up-front model has been, in this author's understanding, less than five.

There are several concerns with the up-front model. First, there are no consumer protection programmes like Green-e to audit the 'give us your money now and we'll build some renewables later' programmes to see if they actually deliver what they promise and if they continue to perform over the 20–30 year project cycle. The collect-the-premiums-up-front model promises to render to consumers a 30-year stream of CO_2 offset benefits in the year the customer makes the payment, essentially counting CO_2 reductions today that will not materialize for as many as 30+ years. This raises a fundamental question of accuracy in environmental claims.

Another risk associated with the collect-the-premiums-up-front model is that future regulation may assign the stream of carbon benefits to an entity other than the REC purchaser (see Clearing the Air, below).

Both methods of making REC payments are worthy of customer purchases. However, it is simply not true that one approach makes the case for additionality better than the other. Additionality simply cannot and should not be determined using a financial yardstick, or on any particular method of financing the project. In addition, the Green-e model of REC payments insures that customers get what they pay for.

In conclusion, renewable energy is the best way (other than energy productivity/efficiency) to reduce GHG emissions. It changes the energy mix and reduces our use of fossil fuels. In many cases, renewable energy is also the least expensive way to reduce GHG emissions. We should be pleased about that and support as much renewable energy generation as we can. The fact that new renewable energy facilities are less expensive to bring on line than other GHG mitigation strategies is no reason to advocate that we not support RECs as GHG offsets; rather, it is a great success story. Instead of customers being stuck with a slow, cumbersome process of supporting renewable energy, RECs and Green-e have made the process simple, transparent and inexpensive: the signs of a functioning marketplace. The market is here and the rules are in place. Let us all participate and move the country to a more renewable and lower carbon future.

Clearing the air: the impact of carbon cap-and-trade regulations on the voluntary market for renewable energy

Robert Harmon

This article first appeared in a modified form in: SOLAR 2006 Conference Proceedings.

Interest in the link between energy and global warming and, consequently, between renewable energy and the reduction of greenhouse gas emissions has grown in recent years. At the same time we have seen the development of a US market in renewable energy certificates, as well as much discussion on the development of regulated and voluntary markets for trading greenhouse gas emission reductions. Legislators and regulators at the federal, state and even local levels are seeking ways to reduce emissions of various air pollutants including CO_2, the leading cause of Global Climate Change. On the west coast, policy makers in California, Oregon and Washington are actively discussing a cap on West Coast CO_2 emissions. In the northeast, at least eight states are engaged in similar policy discussions with the same goal. The EPA estimates that approximately 39 per cent of CO_2 emissions in the US are caused by the production of electricity, and planned additions to capacity are mostly fossil fuel-based; hence there is broad agreement that the reduction of CO_2 from the electricity sector is essential if CO_2 emissions reductions are to occur. In other words, energy consumption, renewable energy, greenhouse gas emissions, and climate change are inextricably linked.

It is therefore not surprising that emerging CO_2 policies at the state level would seem to offer great promise for the renewable energy industry. Most renewable energy generation occurs with near-zero and at times net-negative carbon emissions, making it an attractive technology for those interested in reducing CO_2 emissions. However, the good intentions of legislatures will have little effect on the rate of renewable energy development without proper regulatory mechanisms. Improperly structured regulations could actually eliminate the ability of renewable energy to create emissions reductions.

As mentioned previously, the market for renewable energy can be thought of as two markets: compliance and voluntary. The compliance market is made up of utilities purchasing RECs in order to meet renewable-energy targets set out by state legislatures. The voluntary market is made up of residential, institutional, commercial and industrial customers making voluntary purchases to support 'green' power that drives social and environmental benefits. Discussion here concentrates on the voluntary market, although the compliance market faces many of the same challenges.

What's driving the voluntary market?

Voluntary market purchases are driven in large part by a desire for environmental benefits – often linked to climate change and greenhouse gas emissions. To confirm this, all one needs to do is review the press releases from major green power purchasers. Here are some typical examples:

HSBC Bank (seventh largest US purchaser) (press release): '... HSBC became the world's first major bank to commit to carbon neutrality and today its US banking unit announced that it has offset a substantial quantity of its carbon emissions by purchasing 45,454MWh of clean, wind energy certificates.'

Johnson and Johnson (second largest US purchaser) (company web site): 'We are committed to achieving substantial reductions in CO_2 emissions through such off-site means as purchasing green power and trading carbon emissions credits.'

US General Services Administration (fifth largest US purchaser) (press release): 'Electricity produced from renewable resources reduces the amount of CO_2, a key greenhouse gas, as well as sulfur dioxide (SO_2) and nitrogen oxides (NO_x) into the atmosphere.'

In fact, the vast majority of public announcements regarding corporate or institutional green power purchases make emissions-related claims, particularly with respect to CO_2. When thinking about the potential synergies between the voluntary side of the REC market and the burgeoning voluntary carbon market in the US, it is critical to note the stated environmental motivations of those voluntarily purchasing RECs and to design any future legislation accordingly.

Markets for carbon offsets and RECs hold great potential to support one another in satisfying the public desire to combat climate change in the US if, and only if, future regulations are properly designed.

The vast majority of the pro-renewables legislation recently passed at the state level takes the form of renewable portfolio standards. However, the federal government and states in the west and the northeast are considering additional legislation capping CO_2. The structure and implementation of cap-and-trade-rules will have a dramatic affect on the renewable energy industry and, if implemented incorrectly, may reduce or eliminate the ability of portfolio standards and voluntary customer purchases to reduce CO_2 emissions.

Existing cap-and-trade rules

Under the Clean Air Amendments of 1990, the federal government elected to cap emissions of SO_2 and allow trading of 'allowances' to emit SO_2. The number of allowances allocated was based on the SO_2 intensity of fuel inputs. This is commonly referred to as an input-based system. Virtually all of the allowances were granted to existing emitters. A small number of allowances were set aside for renewables, but the programme was poorly designed and few if any allowances were obtained by renewable energy facilities.[11]

As Figure 3.2 demonstrates, under the input-based cap-and-trade system, the government allocates all allowances to existing emitters. To simplify the explanation, we have assumed a national electricity system requiring 1,000GWh of electricity with a cap on SO_2 of 1,000 tons per year. Hence, each GWh of output requires, on average, one allowance. (Numbers are for example only.)

The result (in this example) is that the two coal plants both operate at capacity, generating a combined 1,000GWhs while emitting 1,000 tons of SO_2.

This system was designed to allow other resources to be added to the grid without increasing the total pollution under the cap. Figure 3.3 demonstrates what happens when the electric load increases by 500GWh per year and that load is met with cleaner natural gas. The emissions cap remains at 1,000 tons.

As Figure 3.3 demonstrates, the government continues to allocate all of the allowances to the coal facilities. In order for the gas plant to produce electricity, it must purchase allowances from the coal facilities. Because the gas plant is cleaner than the coal plant, it only needs to purchase 250 allowances to produce the 500GWhs required. The coal facility can reduce its emissions by 250 tons for less than it will charge the gas plant for the 250 allowances. So it reduces

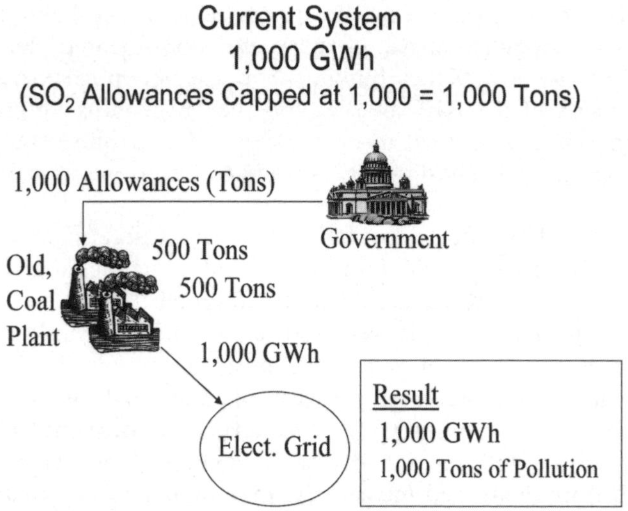

Current System
1,000 GWh
(SO_2 Allowances Capped at 1,000 = 1,000 Tons)

1,000 Allowances (Tons)
Government
Old, Coal Plant
500 Tons
500 Tons
1,000 GWh
Elect. Grid
Result
1,000 GWh
1,000 Tons of Pollution

Figure 3.2 *Current input-based cap-and-trade system*

emissions and sells 250 allowances to the gas plant. The result is that 1,500GWhs are produced and emissions remain at 1,000 tons. The system has accomplished its goals in a cost-effective manner.

It is interesting to observe what happens when a wind facility, rather than a natural gas facility, is used to meet the additional 500GWh load.

In Figure 3.4, the government again allocates all of the allowances to the coal facilities. Because the wind energy facility can produce electricity without emissions, it does not need to purchase allowances from the coal facilities. Therefore, the coal facilities retain all their allowances and make no changes to their emissions. The result is that 1,500GWhs are produced and emissions

Current System
Add 500 GWh with Wind
(Allowances Remain Capped at 1,000)

1,000 Allowances (Tons)
Government
500 Tons
500 Tons
Coal Plant
Makes no changes
1,000 GWh
500 GWh
Elect. Grid
Result
1,500 GWh
Still 1,000 Tons of Pollution

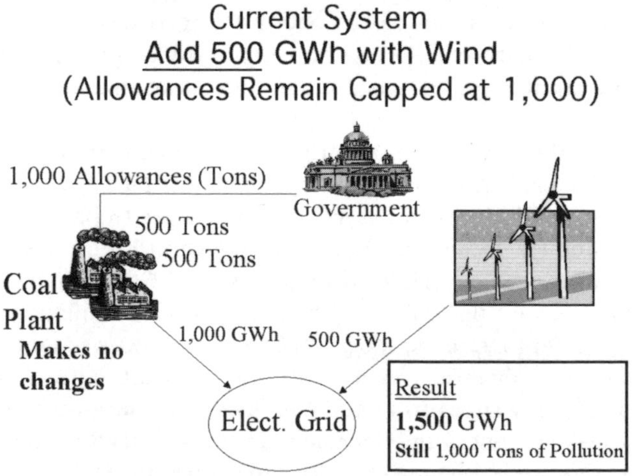

Figure 3.3 *Current system with 500GWh natural gas added*

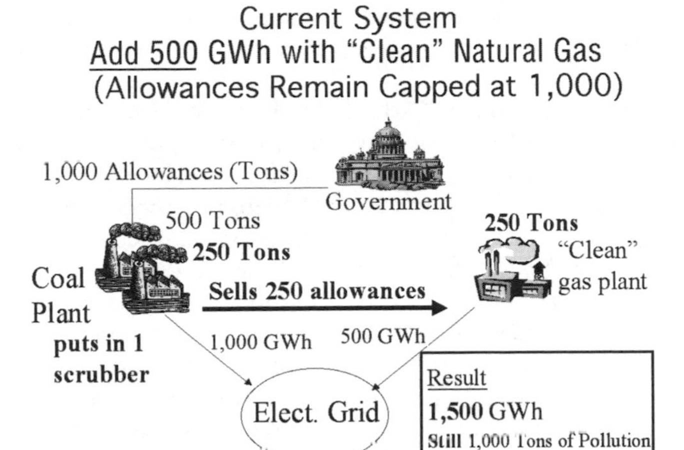

Figure 3.4 *Current system with 500GWh wind added*

remain at 1,000 tons. The system has again accomplished its goals in a cost-effective manner. *However, with regard to total emissions, there is no difference between adding the 500GWhs using the wind facility vs. adding 500GWhs using the gas facility*. In the end, the wind facility can make no claims to have *reduced* SO_2 emissions. Sellers of renewable energy are hence unable to deliver SO_2 reduction benefits to their customers. Under this type of cap-and-trade system, *the amount of SO_2 emitted is not determined by the technology used to generate energy. It is determined by the number of allowances available for use.*

The allowances are valuable *assets* that the emitters will utilize. Emitters receive those allowances even if their facilities shut down. This is an important point, as arguments have been made that once the older facilities shut down, surely society will attain the emissions reductions it desires. Unfortunately, this is not the case. Even if new renewable energy facilities brought enough energy online to shutter an old emitting facility, the said facility would simply sell its allocation of allowances to other remaining emitters, allowing those emitters to increase emissions. For instance, an operating coal plant might purchase allowances from a shuttered facility as a way to postpone pollution equipment maintenance, or it might choose to burn dirtier (and cheaper) coal. In the end, all of the allowances that are available in the marketplace will be used because they have economic value. *The only way to ensure a reduction in pollution under this type of cap-and-trade system is to reduce the number of allowances in the marketplace.*

The risk with CO_2 legislation

Carbon dioxide is not currently regulated under cap-and-trade rules. Therefore, when renewable energy enters the grid and displaces fossil fuels, it does indeed reduce the amount of CO_2 entering the atmosphere. The amount of CO_2 reduction varies from region to region and season to season. But it is clear that less CO_2 is emitted, and it is clear that those reductions are caused by the presence of renewables on the system, displacing fossil-fueled sources that are no longer dispatched.

Emerging legislation on both the federal and state levels to reduce CO_2 emissions is often modeled on SO_2 regulation (an input-based cap-and-trade system). If the SO_2 model is adopted for CO_2, sellers of renewable energy will be unable to deliver CO_2 reduction benefits to their customers, undermining the primary driver for both voluntary and compliance markets. (These sellers may still be able to sell to the regulated entities that require lower-emission energy supplies, but the number of buyers would be smaller and market power would shift from the sellers to buyers: a limited monopsony effect). This is a serious threat to the renewable energy industry.

It is essential that emerging regulations to limit CO_2 emissions recognize the emissions-reduction benefits of renewable energy and allow it to create emissions benefits and deliver them to customers. As states consider CO_2 legislation, the renewable energy community is advocating for such policies.

Output-based cap-and-trade

Output-based cap-and-trade systems are among the alternatives that might be considered. Under an output-based cap-and-trade system, electricity producers are allocated allowances based on their percentage contribution to the grid (in MWhs). If a generator delivers ten per cent of the grid's energy, the generator receives ten per cent of the allowances. As Figure 3.5 demonstrates, a 'clean' natural gas plant provides 500GWh (1/3rd of the total demand) to the grid, while coal facilities provide 1,000GWh (2/3rds). The government therefore allocates 1/3rd of the allowances (333) to the gas plant and 2/3rds (667) to the coal plants.

Because the gas plant operates 'cleanly', it only requires 250 allowances to generate 500GWh. It therefore has 83 allowances available for sale. Those

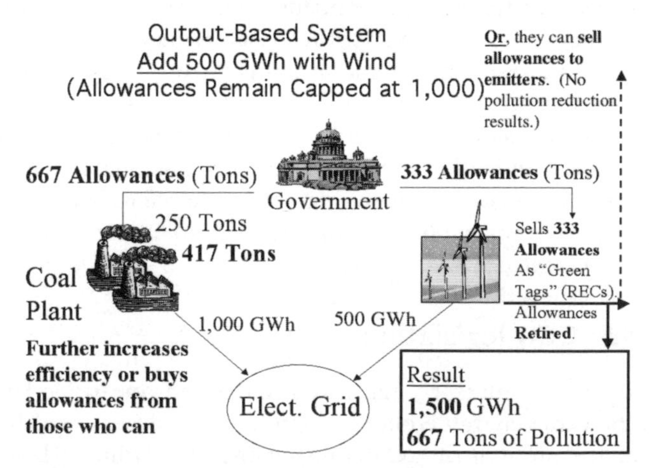

Figure 3.5 *Output-based system with 500GWh natural gas added*

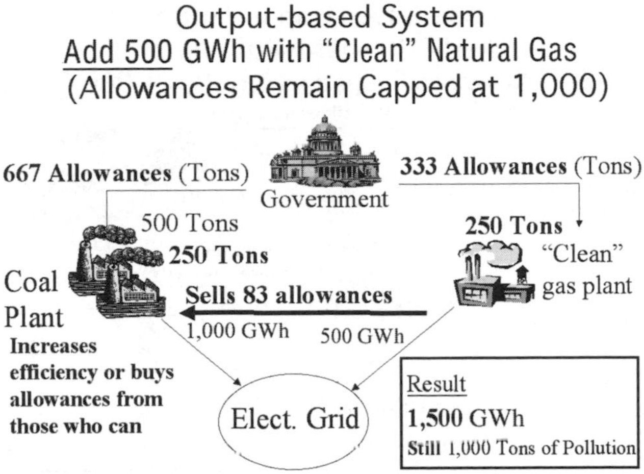

Figure 3.6 *Output-based system with 500GWh of wind added*

allowances are purchased by one of the coal facilities. This leaves the coal facilities with 750 allowances (667 + 83). The coal facility would normally need 1,000 allowances to deliver 1,000GWh to the grid. Therefore, the coal facility will need to reduce its emissions.

It is interesting to observe, in Figure 3.6, what happens when a wind facility rather than a natural gas facility is used to meet the additional 500GWh load.

Again, the government allocates allowances based on the percentage contribution to the grid. The wind facility receives 333 allowances and the coal plants receive 667. Because the wind energy facility can produce electricity without emissions, it does not need to use its allowances to emit. The allowances remain *assets* that the wind facility can use in a variety of ways. It can choose to 'deliver' the allowances as part of a green power product. The product can be delivered to a voluntary customer, or to a compliance customer (a utility, for instance) to meet that customer's regulatory requirement. Either way, the result is that there are 333 fewer allowances available in the marketplace because those allowances are removed from the market when they are sold as green power. This reduction in allowances reduces total emissions, because the coal facilities must reduce emissions further due to the lack of available allowances.

This is precisely the result that both voluntary customers and state regulators desire when they support renewable energy purchases.

The renewable energy facility also has the option of selling the allowances to the coal facilities, which it would be inclined to do if the coal facilities offer a higher price than the voluntary or compliance markets offer. If the wind facility chooses to sell the allowances to the coal facilities, no emissions reductions would result, and the electricity sold by the wind facility would not be considered 'green' in the voluntary market. The energy would also be unlikely to qualify under state renewable energy mandates because a major purpose of those mandates is to reduce emissions, which the wind facility does not accomplish if it sells the allowances to emitting facilities.

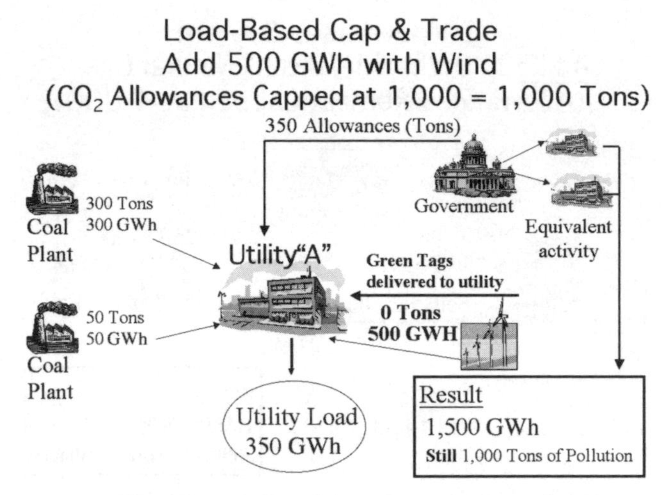

Figure 3.7 *Load-based cap-and-trade*

Allowance set-aside

An allowance set-aside system provides another alternative model. Under an allowance set-aside system for renewables, legislators or regulators set aside a certain number of the total available allowances for new renewable facilities.[12] Thesenew installations apply for the allowances. The result is the same as with an output-based system, however, set-aside systems can be administratively burdensome and treat renewables differently than they treat other generators.

All of the alternatives above are based on capping emissions on the *generation* of electricity. There are alternatives to this approach.

Load-based cap-and-trade

Under a load-based cap-and-trade system, for instance, regulators cap the emissions not of the *generators*, but of the *retail* sellers of electricity. (For the sake of simplicity, we will refer to them as 'utilities'.)

In Figure 3.7, the government sets a total emission cap, *and* a cap on individual utilities. In this case, the emissions of Utility 'A' are capped at 350 tons. The utility purchases 350GWh from 2 coal plants, which emit a total of 350 tons of CO_2.

Figure 3.8 shows what happens when the utility's load increases by 500GWh. The utility cannot purchase additional energy from the coal facilities without exceeding its emissions cap. The logical choice is to purchase from a zero-emissions facility such as a wind farm. The result is that the utility meets its increased load, without exceeding its emissions cap.

Assigning a value to system power

Many utilities purchase a portion of their power in the energy markets, rather than under long-term contracts with specific energy facilities. Given the

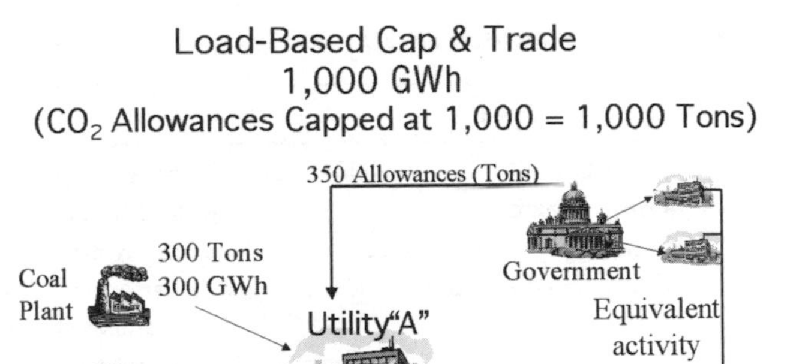

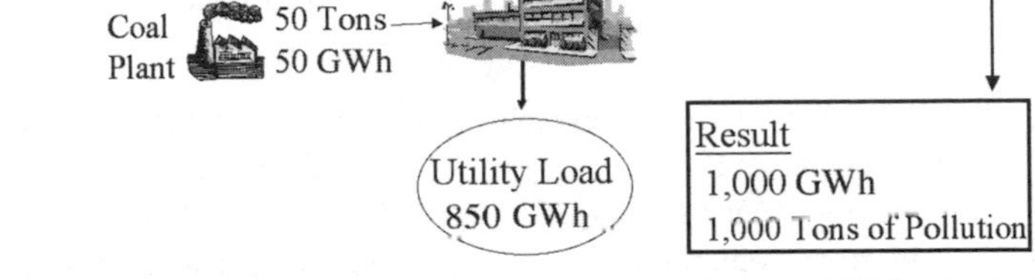

Figure 3.8 *Load-based cap-and-trade with 500GWh of wind added*

fluidity of these markets, it is nearly impossible to know with any certainty the emissions characteristics of system power on a real-time basis. In order to ensure that the emissions associated with utility purchases of system power are counted toward utility emissions caps, it will be necessary for regulators to assign an emissions factor to system power and update it on a regular basis.

When voluntary green power purchases are made under a load-based system, the customers are often purchasing RECs. The result is that the energy remaining after the REC has been sold no longer contains its emissions benefits and must be classified as system power. This prevents the utility purchasing the 'null' energy from counting the emissions benefits already being claimed by the voluntary customer. For the voluntary customer, calculating the emissions benefits associated with their purchase is simple: it is the difference between the emissions characteristics of system power, and those of the renewable energy facility from which the customer purchased the RECs.

The voluntary and compliance markets for renewable energy are growing rapidly. Customers in the voluntary market and legislators passing pro-renewables legislation expect that the new renewable energy added to the grid will improve air quality. SO_2-style (input-based) cap-and-trade regulations eliminate the ability of those parties to achieve those goals. Under a cap-and-trade system, the only way to reduce air pollution for the associated pollutant is to reduce the number of allowances. Without the ability to claim air quality improvements, the demand for new renewable energy will likely be substantially reduced. There are alternatives to the SO_2-style cap-and-trade system that are much more beneficial to renewables and deliver to customers (both voluntary and regulatory) the benefits for which they are willing and in some cases, eager to pay. It is essential for renewable energy industry stakeholders to understand what is at stake and build alliances to ensure that renewable energy can and does continue to deliver to its customers what those customers expect: real environmental benefits. It is also essential that legislators fully

Table 3.4 *Comparison of alternative application systems*

System	Pros	Cons
Output-based	– Direct benefits to renewable energy projects. – Voluntary market creates additional reductions.	– Works poorly for regional cap-and-trade system, increasing costs of local generation and driving utilities to purchase cheaper, dirtier electricity from outside the capped region.
Set-aside	– Direct benefits to renewable energy projects. – Voluntary market creates additional reductions.	– Can be complex and expensive to administer. – Creates burden on clean energy developers who must apply for allowances.
Load-based	– Direct benefits to renewable energy projects. – Voluntary market creates additional reductions. – Pushes utilities to contract with low-emitting suppliers.	– Untried.

understand the impacts of different types of market-based mechanisms on the environment, and how some systems may not deliver the expected environmental benefits. Finally, as regulated and voluntary carbon markets are created in the US, it is important to monitor how these impact existing markets in renewable energy.

Notes

1 World Energy Council, www.worldenergy.org/ accessed in May 2006
2 The US Department of Energy's Green Power Network offers a current list of companies offering certificate-based green power products: www.eere.energy.gov/greenpower/markets/certificate
3 Community Energy Inc. was acquired by IBERDOLA of Spain on 2 May, 2006. www.communityenergy.biz/ accessed in May 2006
4 Green Mountain Energy, 'New Jersey Clean Power Choice Program', www.greenmountain.com/nj/ accessed in June 2006
5 Green-e, renewable electricity certification programme, www.green-e.org/ accessed in June 2006
6 Green-e Verification Report Year 2004, http://green-e.org/pdf/VerificationReport04.pdf
7 Pennock, A. and Doherty, S., Center for Resource Solutions, phone interview June 2006 with W. Wright

8 Environmental Resources Trust Inc., EcoPower SM Program, www.ert.net/ecopower/index.html/ accessed in June 2006
 * For each organization's national standard please see:
 www.green-e.org/pdf/Green-e_National_Standard.v1.pdf
 www.ert.net/pubs/EcoPowerStandard.pdf
9 Kvale, L. Interviewed by Katherine Hamilton March 2006
10 Ibid
11 The federal government also required caps on nitrogen oxides (NO_X) and left many of the implementation details to the states. Space limitations prevent further discussion of the NO_X rules in this paper
12 In order to ensure that emissions reductions occur, it is essential that the allowances that are set aside 'come off the top' of the total number of allowances available. Simply adding the allowances on top of the original allocation would create no net emissions reductions

References

Bird, L. and Swezey, B. (2005) *Green Power Marketing in the US: A Status Report (Eighth Edition)* NREL/TP 620-38994, National Renewable Energy Laboratory, Golden, CO

Gewin, V. (2005) 'What makes energy green? And can it be traded?: Renewable energy and RECs', http://ecosystemmarketplace.com/ accessed in June 2006

Hamilton, K. (2006) 'Navigating the Nebula: Institutional Use of the US Voluntary Carbon Market', Masters Thesis at the Yale School of Forestry and Environmental Studies

Holt, E. and Bird, L. (2005) *Emerging Markets for Renewable Energy Certificates: Opportunities and Challenges* NREL/TP 620-37388, National Renewable Energy Laboratory, Golden, CO

Wright, C. (2006) 'For ABN AMRO, sustainability means business', http://ecosystemmarketplace.com/ accessed in July 2006

Bonneville Environmental Foundation (BEF), www.b-e-f.org/

Websites

ClimateBiz, www.climatebiz.com/
Center for Resource Solutions, www.resource-solutions.org/
Community Energy Inc, www.communityenergy.biz/
Environmental Resources Trust, www.ert.net/
Mainstay Energy, http://mainstayenergy.com/
National Renewable Energy Laboratory, www.nrel.gov/
Native Energy, www.nativeenergy.com/
New Jersey Clean Energy Program, www.njcleanenergy.com/
Sterling Planet, www.sterlingplanet.com/
US Department of Energy's Green Power Network, www.eere.energy.gov
World Energy Council, www.worldenergy.org/
3 Phases Energy Services, www.3phases.com

4

The Voluntary Carbon Market: What the Experts Think

Now that we understand how the voluntary carbon market functions today, we are in a position to consider how it will operate in the future. Since we are in full agreement with Mark Twain, who once quipped that, 'prophecy is a good line of business, but it is full of risks,' we have decided not to make all the predictions ourselves. In this chapter, then, we have asked a series of experts to take a close look at current market trends and to make predictions about what the future holds for the voluntary carbon market.

The following ten editorials represent a wide range of perspectives from a wide range of participants – read on to find out what scientists and investors, project developers and policymakers, communities and corporations, retailers and conservationists think about the voluntary carbon markets of today and tomorrow.

An economist's perspective on the voluntary carbon market: Useful but not sufficient

Janet Peace

When trying to understand the relationship between regulated carbon markets, voluntary carbon markets, and the larger global fight against climate change, it is important to bear in mind two things: (1) Voluntary efforts alone, although important, will not sufficiently reduce greenhouse gas (GHG) emissions, and (2) Since the US is the largest emitter of these gases, accounting for approximately 23 per cent of global emissions, no meaningful regulatory effort can succeed without the country's involvement. Bearing these facts in mind, we can now turn to look at what is happening in the US vis-à-vis carbon markets, and voluntary carbon markets in particular.

Although the US does not currently have a mandatory climate programme, a voluntary market for carbon has developed. This market includes industries, project developers, consumers, several registries and even a trading exchange

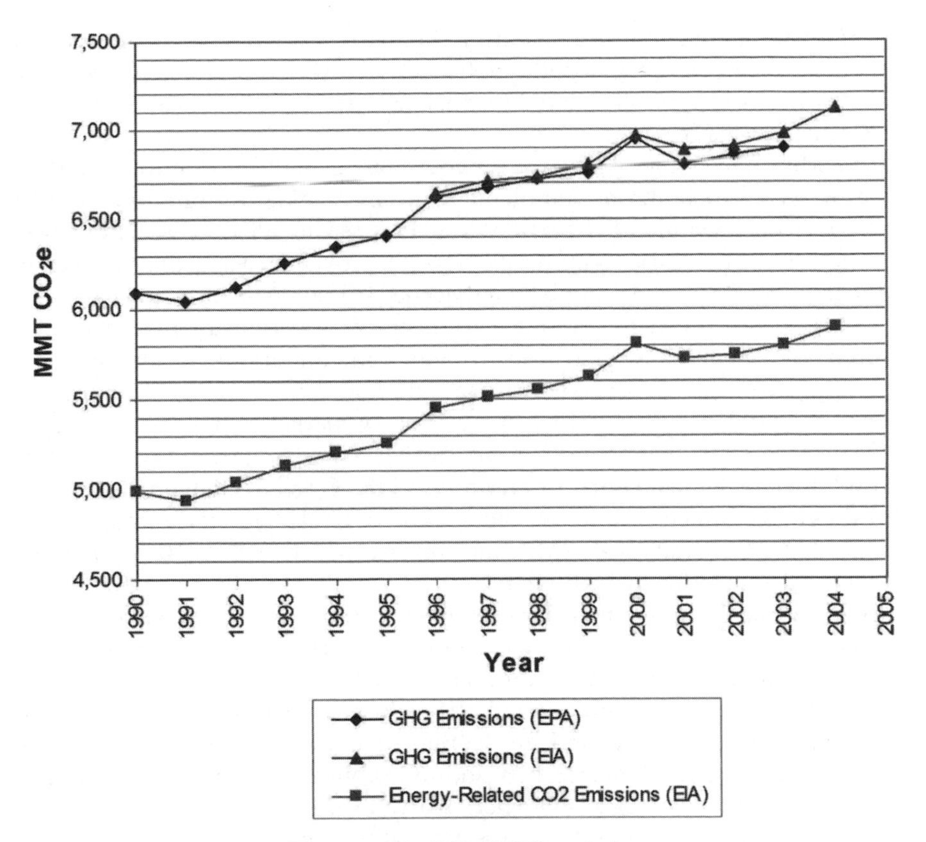

Figure 4.1 *US GHG emissions*

(the Chicago Climate Exchange, or CCX). Without a mandatory federal programme that imposes specific reduction requirements, however, this voluntary GHG market does not have enough demand, supply, consistency, or infrastructure to address the challenge we face from climate change fully.

It is clear that voluntary efforts are not enough because we have had a voluntary programme in the US now for several years and emissions continue to rise at an alarming rate. Since 1990 they have increased 18 per cent, even though President Bush established a voluntary emissions intensity target of 18 per cent improvement (emissions per unit of output) in 2002.

Although incapable of achieving the levels of emission cuts needed, voluntary markets are important and can aid in addressing the challenge of climate change in a number of ways. First, they can act as an important precursor to a mandatory emissions-trading programme by educating stakeholders (including policymakers and firms) about emission reduction opportunities, measurement tools and infrastructure requirements. Industry also benefits from learning about trading and risk management in a voluntary market because prices are likely lower than they would be under a mandatory system. The Chicago Climate Exchange (CCX) provides a good example of this. It promotes membership by noting that participation builds 'the practical skills needed to manage and trade GHG emissions' and it is noteworthy that participants have typically paid less than $5 per metric ton of CO_2 since CCX began operating.[1]

In addition to being a precursor for compliance markets, voluntary markets can also act as a significant complement to any mandatory programme. For instance, where voluntary reductions can be used as offsets for compliance, they help increase market depth and liquidity (by increasing the number of suppliers who can provide supply when needed). The use of offsets in a mandatory market also broadens the financial incentive for innovation to firms not covered by regulations; and can provide an important mechanism for containing the costs associated with meeting mandatory targets. In addition, the general public can participate in a voluntary market to purchase offsets to cover their own GHG emissions – again further expanding the scope of trading beyond that of a mandatory programme. The Oregon Climate Trust and TerraPass (see appendices at the back of this book) are, for example, two groups that offer individuals the ability to buy GHG offsets to compensate for their own travel related emissions.

And, while there is much discussion in this book and elsewhere on the relationship between mandatory and voluntary carbon markets, in my view, implementation of a mandatory programme with targets and clearly defined rules will only improve and expand the voluntary market. Mandatory and voluntary programmes can and do operate together. The recent transaction between the Oregon Climate Trust and 3C (Climate Change Consulting in Frankfurt, Germany) is clear evidence that the two markets can exist side by side. 3C operates in a country with a mandatory carbon trading programme under Kyoto Protocol rules (which specifically disallow reductions from non-Kyoto parties like the US) yet they still purchased voluntary US reductions. These tons were not used to fulfill compliance obligations but rather to provide carbon-neutral strategies like offsetting the emissions from the FIFA Football World Cup 2006. Purchases for noncompliance by industry and the general public are a small but growing niche market for carbon reductions.

In the US today, we do not have a mandatory national climate programme and consequently, the only sources of demand for carbon in the country are: these developing niche markets; a couple of voluntary federal programmes which encourage industrial GHG reductions; and the few state programmes that require GHG offsets for new power plants.[2] The end result is that today's US GHG market is primarily voluntary, with few buyers, few sellers, low prices, limited transparency and limited consistency among those participating in the market. Lack of transparency and consistency can also raise doubts about whether efforts are benefiting the environment – the issue is specifically whether reduction efforts being bought and sold on these markets are credible.

Credibility is a vital issue for all carbon markets and its significance cannot be overstated. Without some level of consumer understanding and confidence that trading is not a shell game, there is little chance of developing the political will necessary to set up a mandatory GHG trading system, let alone a trading system that would use voluntary project-based reductions (offsets).

One possible way to improve and expand the credibility of current efforts, prior to the introduction of government imposed rules, would be to develop a widely agreed upon and consistent definition of what constitutes a GHG offset or carbon credit. A consistent definition and some type of branding would help buyers (and ultimately sellers) of voluntary reductions understand what they are buying, in much the same way that the Energy Star label in the US has helped consumers recognize and select energy-efficient appliances. This need for consistency and credibility has been recognized by participants in the voluntary market, including CCX, WRI, the Climate Group, Climate Wedge, the California Climate Action Registry, and others who have attempted to create a credible definition. To date, however, the definition of an offset is still not uniform and buyers must closely scrutinize the quality of their carbon purchases.

So where does this leave us? What will happen by 2010? Will the carbon market be truly global? While this is both desirable and a possibility, 2010 is only four short years away. By then we may first see development of some new regulated carbon markets in several regions throughout the US, and these may or may not be linked to each other. Over time (and how long this time-frame will be, is hard to say), these regional markets will likely be expanded to become a national programme and then – some time after that – this national market may establish close links with international markets. However they develop, one thing is clear – a mandatory programme is necessary to the development of a fully functioning carbon market. And while voluntary efforts are useful, they should be seen only as a precursor and complement to regulated markets, never as a substitute. Alone they will never be sufficient.

A conservationist's perspective on the voluntary carbon market: Can it help us overcome inertia?

Ben Vitale

Climate change is such a dire problem that, if we are to tackle it, optimism, entrepreneurial innovation, steadfast conviction, and systematic changes in global social and economic infrastructure must be combined in amounts never before orchestrated. We need the visionary oversight of policy makers, the innovation of the private sector, and the hope and conviction of all global citizens.

By putting a price on the activities that lead to climate change, carbon markets can help knit together the activities of businesses, consumers and policymakers on all sides of the world. Unfortunately, deploying global policy takes decades, and will only be effective when all countries and individuals adopt the most stringent greenhouse gas reduction targets. Today's regulatory markets do not come close to substantially reducing the potential impacts of dangerous levels of climate change at or below the 450 parts per million (PPM) that many scientists advise.

Voluntary carbon markets thus have an important role to play in the coming years: As we enter a transition period between lax regulation and the sort of drastic reductions that are needed to address climate change, voluntary markets can move us to adopt innovative climate change solutions more quickly.

Voluntary markets are not as constrained as the regulated markets, so a key role for these markets should be to push innovation and fund creative solutions ahead of regulation. Projects funded by the voluntary market must be of high quality and they must deliver measurable emissions reductions, but this does not necessarily mean that only regulated modalities should be considered. For example, the current regulated markets place land-use projects at a disadvantage by excluding the emissions that result from deforestation completely and by limiting the amount of land-use-based credits that countries may purchase.

Strongly supporting emissions reductions from avoided deforestation and active forest restoration allows the voluntary carbon market to yield many benefits. These include:

- Time to pursue alternative technology and development pathways in the short term;
- Support for the major goals of the Convention on Biological Diversity (CBD), the Ramsar Convention on Wetlands of International Importance, and The Convention on the Conservation of Migratory Species of Wild Animals, to protect threatened biodiversity, as an important contribution to poverty alleviation;
- A revenue source for impoverished developing countries that are carbon- and biodiversity-rich; and
- Opportunities to reduce poverty by furthering the Millennium Development Goals (MDGs).

This emphasis on tangible projects accruing multiple benefits (i.e. carbon reductions, biodiversity conservation and poverty alleviation) with broad stakeholder engagement is particularly important because climate change is occurring during, and contributing to, the sixth-largest species extinction spasm ever documented.

There are many multiple-benefit projects that must sell both certified and voluntary carbon offsets in order to be financially viable. One such project is the Mantadia-Zahamena Corridor Restoration and Protection Project in Madagascar (see box). This project seeks to produce Kyoto CDM-certified emissions reductions, voluntary emissions reductions produced by avoiding the burning of tropical forest, biodiversity protection and community sustainable livelihoods. The project expects to obtain as much as one third of the required project financing from the regulated and voluntary carbon trading markets.

Lastly, voluntary markets have a unique role to play in heightening consumer awareness of climate change, its threats and its solutions. The world needs action and commitment – in other words, sacrifice – from citizens on a scale not experienced in many decades, if ever. The voluntary markets, when coupled with strict regulations, can help drive the early action, entrepreneurial innovation, increased consumer awareness and engagement necessary to stabilize greenhouse gas concentrations in the atmosphere. In particular, voluntary markets can help citizens in developed countries understand how they might assist those communities in developing countries that are especially vulnerable to the impacts of climate change.

Growing voluntary markets in a regulated world

While voluntary markets are an important means of combating climate change for all of the reasons just cited, they should in no way be seen as an alternative to regulation. For this reason, some argue that voluntary markets are superfluous and that they will cease to exist once regulated markets emerge.

If global and regional regulations provided a completely closed system capable of accounting for global emissions from all sources, these critics of voluntary markets would probably be right. Regulatory markets would displace voluntary markets or, at least, reduce them dramatically. This scenario, however, is not likely to become a reality for at least another few decades, and it may never happen. Even if countries like the US, Canada, and Australia implemented carbon cap-and-trade schemes tomorrow, the regulations guiding these schemes would probably be limited in scope, leaving many emitting sectors out of the market. And if the regulated markets become very fragmented – with each country adopting its own rules – then the line may blur between the voluntary and regulated markets in any event. For these reasons, I think the voluntary market may not peak for decades.

Whatever happens in the next decade, it is probably safe to say that the voluntary carbon markets will be larger in 2010 and 2020 than they are now. Since the magnitude of global climate change is so large, and the current pace of policy interventions is so slow, voluntary carbon markets could transact hundreds of millions – even billions – of dollars annually before truly effective compliance carbon markets are up and running at the scale we need.

In the meantime, governments may develop innovative bilateral or multilateral agreements outside traditional emissions markets that may boost investments in projects that might be considered 'voluntary'. For example, developing countries with significant emissions from deforestation and other land-use change could provide government-backed rainforest credits by adopting a voluntary cap on emissions from the forestry and land-use sectors outside of any regulatory regime. Developing countries, meanwhile, could obtain incentives to leapfrog older high emitting technologies if bilateral agreements and funding were deployed effectively. These mechanisms might provide significant incentives for consumers, institutions and non-regulated businesses to take voluntary action in ways that would grow the market.

Clearly, governments, scientists and the private sector must continually search for new ways to unlock creativity and entrepreneurship to address climate change. Governments need to enact climate legislation, but they must also provide incentives to help speed the adoption of new lower-emissions technologies. Businesses are quickly learning how they can become climate friendly while turning a profit. For example, some leadership companies such as ST Microelectronics, DuPont, Ricoh Corporation, HSBC, Swiss Re and others have already taken on voluntary commitments that go beyond their regulated obligations.

Change, it seems, is happening, but it needs to happen more quickly and on a larger scale. Fortunately, there is room for hope: When John Doerr and Vinod Khosla – the venture capitalists who first backed global giants such as Google and Sun Microsystems – and other investors begin funding new green technologies, it is a strong signal that the gloves have come off, and entrepreneurs are ready to begin developing solutions that make both commercial and environmental sense in this carbon-constrained world.

Box 4.1 Case Study: Mantadia-Zahamena Corridor Restoration and Protection Project, Republic of Madagascar

The Mantadia-Zahamena Corridor Restoration and Protection Project is conducting native forest restoration and protection activities with two primary goals:

(1) to establish natural forest corridors that allow viable biological connectivity among several currently isolated high biodiversity forests and protected areas; and
(2) to promote sustainable cultivation systems to increase soil fertility, protect watersheds, and stabilize land-use to reduce deforestation in the 405,000 hectare corridor. These activities will significantly increase forest cover and reduce deforestation, sequestering and avoiding approximately 17 million tons CO_2.

These activities are being carried out in conjunction with local communities, government agencies and other stakeholders. Specific actions include:

- Increasing forest cover by avoiding deforestation, reconnecting the fragmented landscape, and restoring degraded lands to functioning ecosystems;
- Developing new agricultural and forestry techniques to improve productivity of degraded zones and provide new alternatives to farmers and communities;

- Building local capacity in Madagascar to implement climate change initiatives including technical, implementation, financial and legal aspects;
- Promoting project benefits to (1) purchasers of compliance and voluntary emissions reductions who provide project financing, and (2) donors and funding agencies interested in supporting community livelihoods and biodiversity conservation benefits;
- Using proven methodologies, monitoring techniques, remote sensing, and aerial photography to assess forest change at the national level.

A project developer's perspective on the voluntary carbon market: Carbon sequestration in the Sierra Gorda of Mexico

David Patrick Ross and Martha Isabel Ruiz Corzo

Bosque Sustentable, A.C., a nongovernmental organization working in the Sierra Gorda Biosphere Reserve and its area of influence in eastern central Mexico, signed a contract in March 2006 with the United Nations Foundation for the sale of 5,230 emission reduction units (tCO_2e). The contract was the culmination of years of hard work, and our experience with the international carbon market during this time highlights the difficulties and opportunities for organizations interested in developing carbon sequestration projects in areas of poverty.

The Sierra Gorda Biosphere Reserve is located in the Sierra Madre Oriental mountain range in the northern extreme of the State of Queretaro. With a total surface area of 383,567 hectares (32 per cent of the State's territory), the Reserve has 11 core zones of 24,803 hectares and a buffer zone of 358,764 hectares.

Located in a transition zone between the Nearctic and Neotropical biogeographical regions, the Reserve constitutes the most ecosystem-diverse natural protected area in Mexico. The 15 vegetation types found within the Reserve's boundaries include semi-desert scrub, temperate forests of pines and oaks, cloud forests, dry tropical forests and tropical rain forests. Ranking second among Mexico's natural protected areas in terms of biodiversity, the Sierra Gorda is home to species of Mexican felines including the jaguar, puma, bobcat, margay, ocelot and jaguarundi.

Despite its natural riches, the Reserve is an area of severe poverty. Approximately 100,000 inhabitants live in 638 localities throughout the Reserve and four of the five municipalities are ranked as highly marginalized. The fifth is ranked as very highly marginalized. To give you a sense of the level of poverty about which we are speaking, it is worth noting that more than 70 per cent of the economically active population in Pinal de Amoles, the site of carbon sequestration for the UN Foundation, makes less than US$8.00 per day.

Bosque Sustentable, founded in 2002, works in close coordination with the management of the Sierra Gorda Biosphere Reserve and with its civil society partner organization, Grupo Ecologico Sierra Gorda. From 1998–2004 the organizations of the Sierra Gorda focused their carbon efforts on looking for opportunities to enter the carbon market created by the Kyoto Protocol.

An uphill battle

The barriers we encountered when trying to enter the Clean Development Mechanism of Kyoto are common to many areas of poverty located in Mexico and throughout Latin America. At the most basic level, they include the lack of capital for developing projects, and the lack of forest management skills among local landholders. Even when local capacity has been developed, high costs for verification and certification of emission reductions can result in more carbon money going into the hands of consultants from other countries than to local people planting and protecting trees.

Another important barrier is the pattern of land ownership in the Sierra Gorda, which lacks large, compact properties. Bosque Sustentable works with small landholders with an average plantation size of one hectare. This means that for a project of 500 hectares – small by international standards – Bosque Sustentable must work with approximately 500 different landholders scattered throughout the mountains. These properties lack telephone service and are accessible only by hours of driving on rough unpaved roads, dramatically increasing the per-unit costs of carbon sequestration. In addition, the majority of landholders do not hold title to the property in their own name. In most cases, the title to the property is in the name of a deceased relative and although possession is not in dispute, legal costs and exorbitant notary fees prevent the landholders from updating the titles.

Not surprisingly, impoverished farmers require payments in the early years of the plantations, prior to the onset of sustainable harvesting. Although government programmes support tree planting, mortality is high, and the payments are increasingly insufficient to attract participation. Carbon sales provide an additional incentive for participation, as well as small payments to landholders who otherwise simply cannot afford the investment of time and resources to establish and ensure the survival of a plantation. Although some buyers in the CDM market will make up-front investments, the additional risk involved usually entails a lower purchase price.

The unresolved issue of additionality was also difficult for us to navigate as a community project in a rural area. With the support of an international consultant with CDM experience, Bosque Sustentable argues that although its project includes lands located within a federal Natural Protected Area (NPA), the lands are private and there is no legal requirement for reforestation; therefore, the CDM requirement for project additionality can be met. Other consultants and certain nongovernmental organizations, however, continue to argue that reforestation within NPAs should not be considered 'additional' for CDM purposes.

For these reasons and others, Bosque Sustentable and its partner organizations decided to leave behind their efforts to enter the CDM market. 'For years we heard that the Clean Development Mechanism was a tool for sustainable development,' explains Martha Isabel Ruiz Corzo, director of the Sierra Gorda Biosphere Reserve. 'The reality is that the CDM is light years away from the needs of areas of poverty.'

A better fit

Now Bosque Sustentable is focusing on the voluntary carbon market. Its programme of Carbon Sequestration for Sustainable Forestry in the Sierra Gorda Biosphere Reserve is targeted to organizations, businesses and individuals that not only want to contribute to the fight against global warming, but that also want to fight poverty and conserve biodiversity.

This Sierra Gorda carbon sequestration project, developed with the assistance of Woodrising Consulting, Inc. and the 'Biodiversity Conservation in the Sierra Gorda Biosphere Reserve' project (supported by the Global Environment Facility), sequesters carbon by reforesting lands previously converted to agricultural and livestock uses in the Sierra Gorda Biosphere Reserve and its area of influence in the state of San Luis Potosi. The project fights poverty through the creation of numerous small-scale landholder-managed plantations. Participants include private and communal landowners, as well as landholders when there is no dispute regarding possession (as indicated by a record of possession obtained from the local municipal authority). All participants must sign contracts committing to the management of their plantations for carbon sequestration for 30 years and transferring the legal right to emission reductions to Bosque Sustentable.

The sale of emission reductions provides the financial incentives needed to obtain and maintain landowner participation until the plantations reach sufficient maturity to provide the landowners with income from sustainable harvesting. These incentives are backed by a coordinated effort, implemented by a team of community organizers and forestry experts, to organize the landowners into well-equipped professional associations that provide them with professional training on silvicultural techniques, sustainable forestry management, wood transformation technologies, product development and marketing, and business management. The project preserves old-growth forests by discouraging their use for wood and instead makes regulated plantations the primary source of wood for the region.

As structured, the project requires up-front payments from buyers for the sequestration of carbon during a project life of 30 years. Emission reduction credits are issued every five years following verification. Although specific properties are identified for the generation of the emission reductions for each individual sale, Bosque Sustentable maintains the flexibility to substitute emission reductions from similar properties as needed. In addition, Bosque Sustentable retains 20 percent of the projected emissions reductions as a form of self-insurance.

The sale to the UN Foundation of 5,230 emission reduction credits is the first for the project. As part of its commitment to carbon neutral operations, the UN Foundation used the methodology of the GHG protocol and tools provided by the World Resources Institute to calculate the total amount of its historical carbon dioxide emissions from electricity consumption, heating and cooling, and air travel at its Washington, D.C. and New York offices. With pro bono legal services generously proved by Baker & McKenzie, the UN Foundation then purchased an equivalent amount of carbon offsets from Bosque Sustentable, which received the assistance of the Mexican Center for Environmental Law.

The Sierra Gorda experience shows that the voluntary carbon market has the potential to play an important role in sustainable development efforts around the world. To achieve this potential, however, the development of rigid Kyoto-like standards for the voluntary market must be avoided. Instead, flexible but reliable criteria should be utilized to meet the needs of areas of severe poverty.

A policy perspective on the voluntary carbon market: Seeding a real market for emissions reductions

Ben Henneke

Whether through barter, clam shells, or debit cards, mankind has been using 'real' markets – voluntary markets – to improve both physical and psychological quality-of-life for millennia. Experience shows that markets increase choice, create abundance, develop technology, and create 'win–win' situations for both buyer and seller. Real markets develop where there is actual demand, and freedom to meet that demand in a number of ways.

To date, regulatory markets have reduced the cost of compliance and enforcement, but they have failed to deliver other expected environmental benefits: specifically, rapid reductions in pollution loadings, and rapid technological development and deployment. They have also failed to provide a reliable 'cost of compliance' as originally expected. For example, over the past decade, the US sulfur dioxide (SO_2, or SOx) market price has varied over 1500 per cent, while the regional nitrous oxide (or NOx) market has fluctuated by over 300 per cent, and the California Reclaim set a record by moving over 120,000 per cent. 'Real' markets have not exhibited such wild fluctuations in the thousands of years they have existed (the US stock market crashes of 1939 and 1987, for instance, led to fluctuations of just 24 per cent).

So, are environmental markets a disaster? Should they be abandoned for some form of command and control or technology forcing approach that mandates what technology must be used? I don't think so. I think that all we need to do is to back up a little, and learn from all the successful markets that have existed, and then fix our environmental markets to be like them. So, briefly, let's back up.

Let's get real

If we really want to make substantial progress on environmental issues – if we want to encourage technology, creativity, variety, and reasonable costs, and we want those results fast – then we need to harness the proven power of 'real' markets in order to achieve our environmental objectives. Importantly, I think the evolving voluntary carbon market provides us with an opportunity to start doing just this. But before I tout the voluntary carbon market's important role in advancing us toward a real environmental market in emissions reductions, let me say upfront that I do not think the market will ever really take off in the absence of a regulatory driver.

Some (not many) market observers believe that people having information about environmental needs (such as the threat of climate change) will force changes in technology and business practice without any regulations or requirements. Some successes have been recorded using this approach: for example, the Toxics Release Inventory programme in the US, which only requires that industries report the quantity of various toxic substances released to the environment, has reduced by nearly half the number of toxics reported. But, for many people, the idea that all of mankind will suddenly begin to do the right environmental thing on a voluntary basis seems somewhat Utopian.

Fortunately, more widespread regulation is probably on the way when it comes to the emission of carbon dioxide. The scientific demand for emission reductions far outstrips the current global supply, and institutions throughout the world have begun agitating for political action on the issue of climate change. And while we wait for widespread carbon regulation, the voluntary carbon market has much to teach us about how to create a 'real' supply of emission reductions.

Unlike cap-and-trade schemes, trading allowances between participants acting as both buyers and sellers, buyers on the voluntary carbon market generally contract with unregulated suppliers to purchase carbon credits through project-based transactions. These suppliers and the carbon credits they generate come in all stripes and sizes and this, I would argue, is the great strength of the voluntary carbon market. Creating supply – creating sellers – is the real opportunity for the voluntary carbon market.

A critical period

Unlike the compliance carbon market where the supply of carbon offset projects is constrained by the strict methodologies and bureaucracy of the Clean Development Mechanism (CDM), supply in the voluntary carbon market comes from all kinds of projects in all kinds of countries. In large part because international policymakers have ignored it, the voluntary carbon market has been left alone to work out which types of projects it will support. And as long as there is assurance that credits will be audited to guarantee adequate quality, this is as it should be.

Now that the compliance market has boomed to unforeseen levels and new buyers are looking at the voluntary carbon market more closely, there has been a sudden international push to standardize supply in the voluntary carbon market. I believe that this push represents both a dangerous risk and an important opportunity for the market.

If centralized bodies get involved in dictating which types of projects should be allowed into the voluntary carbon market and which should not, I believe they will strangle supply and hurt both buyers (who will face inflated prices) and sellers (who will face inflated project costs). Sadly, the impoverished communities who stand ready to become suppliers of emission reductions in rural areas where the voluntary carbon market's revenues are needed most, will be the first to be shut out of the market.

If, however, the voluntary market can develop an accounting methodology that fuels consumer confidence in the market, but does not strangle the widely varied and innovative sources of supply currently emerging, then it will have moved the world one huge step toward the creation of a real market for carbon emission reductions – one in which demand is regulated by a central body, but supply is not.

Cost-effective and credible

As institutions and individuals become increasingly informed about how carbon markets operate, they will also become increasingly choosy when it comes to selecting the carbon offsets they wish to purchase. Projects that cannot demonstrate to consumers that the offsets they are selling are both cost-effective and credible will go out of business. Projects that can prove they are selling verifiable emission reductions at competitive prices will succeed. And projects that can differentiate themselves by showing that the offsets they generate not only reduce GHGs in the atmosphere but also help communities and natural ecosystems in the process, will capture those consumers who wish to pay the highest prices for the rarest form of credit.

Working with subsistence farmers in East Africa and India to help them certify The International Small Group and Tree Planting Program (TIST) project with the CDM has taught me a great deal about which transaction costs are real and necessary to provide consumers with confidence in the product they are buying and which are not.

At TIST, we set out to marry Western accounting practices with East African and Indian cultures and realities. Using a global positioning system (GPS) and a personal digital assistant (PDA), subsistence farmers can now send the coordinates and measurements of the trees they have planted to investors in Washington D.C. or London from tree groves in the middle of rural

India or Africa. The TIST website lists the precise latitude and longitude of each farmer's grove and tracks the number of trees and seedlings that are planted, helping drive accountability to western investors. Third-party verifiers check that the recorded data lines up with what is happening on the ground, and regular accounting reports are prepared and filed.

All of the myriad costs associated with this tracking and accounting system, I would argue, are necessary to ensure real environmental benefits and long-term customer satisfaction. Filing endless paperwork with a single centralized body and then waiting for the project to inch forward through a tangle of bureaucracy step by step is not only unnecessary, but also inimical to the goal of reducing emissions quickly and effectively.

My experience with TIST, then, has convinced me that the common standard to which all projects must aspire is simple: they must provide what they advertise, any carbon offsets they sell must be verified by a third party as measurable and real, and they must record and track transactions in a registry that is transparent and well monitored. Beyond that, I say we let the buyers decide which projects they will support, and which they will not.

Will there be cheats in the system? Will there be scandals? Will some projects advertise themselves falsely? Yes, yes and oh yes. But we must remember that a real and robust market will, eventually, weed out the bad apples from the good. Importantly, the voluntary carbon market is already providing an arena in which this important process can begin to take place. Registries have already cropped up in several places and efforts to rank offset providers are now underway. Large institutional buyers have learned how to ask the tough questions of the suppliers from whom they buy credits, and individuals, I think, won't be far behind.

If the voluntary market can pioneer a new strategy for ensuring real and innovative sources of supply, then it is my firm belief that the world, at last, will be poised to launch a successful environmental market capable of addressing global climate change.

The real thing

A real carbon market – a hybrid of the compliance and voluntary carbon markets we see today – would boast a broad requirement for reductions, and it would make sure the requirements grow over time. Then, once regulators had created demand in this market through widespread regulation, they would stand back to be thrilled as companies competed to purchase the best quality reductions and hundreds, even thousands, of suppliers competed to make ever-better real reductions.

This hypothetical market may sound like a bit of a pipe dream today, but that may soon change if the voluntary carbon market can help us come up with a better way to supply carbon credits. We stand at a moment in history when we can learn from our past mistakes with environmental markets and then create something that is newer, better and more effective. Let's not blow the chance.

A retailer's perspective on the voluntary carbon market: Voluntary action obligatory for effective strategy on emissions

Jonathan Shopley

As Einstein said, every action has an equal and opposite reaction. So, with climate change finally hitting the top of the global political agenda, could 2006 be the year an effective reaction to prevent its potentially devastating affects will finally be set in motion?

Some fear it is already too late: The new global consensus on the '60 per cent imperative' – that only a 60 per cent reduction in global emissions will divert us from effects of a truly catastrophic nature – is balanced by the reality that emissions are rising at a faster rate than ever. The world cannot wait any longer.

Against that backdrop the voluntary carbon market has a vital role to play, because if global warming emissions are to be tackled rigorously and immediately, reliance on the compliance carbon market will not suffice. Only the expansion of the voluntary carbon market has the capacity to bypass the naturally cumbersome progress of a regulatory approach and make up the difference between regulated reductions, which on their own will be too little too late.

Steven Pacala and Robert Socolow at Princeton University recently introduced the climate 'stabilization wedge' – a 'unit' for discussing effective emissions reduction activity – and suggested that 'implementing seven wedges' should put us on the right course. The voluntary market leverages a number of wedges – enabling participation in this market by sectors, companies and individuals that might otherwise have been left out.

Closing the gap, these scientists correctly suggest, will require a variety of behavioural shifts, alongside the development and implementation of new technologies. Can the voluntary carbon market rise to the challenge?

In its favour is its ability to deliver rapid results, by providing a process for organizations to assess their own carbon footprint and independently implement effective reduction or offsetting activities.

The evolving corporate response

Companies – particularly UK corporates – are increasingly well educated on climate change issues, and also on the potential benefits of a CarbonNeutral approach to running their business.

The ever-growing importance of corporate reputation management, for instance, means more scrutiny from shareholders and NGOs of companies' carbon management processes. In this sense voluntary action can help increase stakeholder trust in a brand or business. Media and consumer power means that poor reputation has the potential to damage a company financially, and in this context voluntary action on carbon emissions is becoming an increasingly important part of risk management strategy.

But voluntary carbon management is not just a defensive commercial weapon. Reducing emissions generally means increasing efficiency, with good carbon management practice ultimately showing positive benefits to the bottom line. It can even support commercial partnerships and the winning of new business, as companies carrying a visible and credible CarbonNeutral brand will increasingly seek peers whose carbon concerns not only reflect their own, but can assist them in meeting their own carbon targets – greening the supply chain in the process.

Carbon management can also benefit a business in terms of staff commitment, providing opportunities to boost engagement and retention by demonstrating environmental values and by enabling staff to take part in the company's CarbonNeutral activities.

In fact, with the business reasons for taking action strengthening all the time, it is increasingly the large companies who are leading the charge in the expansion of the voluntary carbon market. In our work delivering end-to-end carbon management services, The CarbonNeutral Company has witnessed these effects in some of the world's largest companies – and not just as short-term initiatives.

BSkyB has committed to a five-year CarbonNeutral programme; Avis is in its fifth year of being a CarbonNeutral company; and HSBC has an ongoing commitment tied to its primary interest of carbon financing. Companies taking a leadership position are using voluntary routes to go beyond mere regulatory compliance, recognizing that the uncertainty of what will happen in the regulated market after 2012, when the current Kyoto agreements comes to an end, is impacting strategic and investment decisions.

Little wonder they should be driving carbon reduction activity through the voluntary carbon market. Corporate players have also positively influenced the way the voluntary market operates, not least with the move away from a simple 'tree planting' mentality to sophisticated renewable energy and energy efficiency projects frequently linked to the sustainable development of communities in developing countries.

Enabling growth

Corporate engagement is one of the key enablers for the voluntary carbon market to now expand in the way it must to fulfill its potential. The UK is one of the world's most climate-aware countries, with London emerging as the centre for the international carbon market, and London-based companies – a disproportionately high number of which appear on the Carbon Leaders Index – lobbying for stronger action on climate change. The communication of these actions, combined with rising levels of information from the Government and media, is driving awareness and essential behaviour change.

Government also has a massive incentivizing role to play giving positive financial or brand endorsement to voluntary action. A regime for rewarding 'beyond compliance' actions – such as tax incentives or an amended depreciation schedule – would help to both complement and support the slower compliance market and would probably prove quicker and more effective for Government to put in place than the lengthy re-engineering of the existing regulatory structure.

With UK Government backing, the engagement of companies taking a leadership position on voluntary action could be unstoppable, not just encouraging their own programmes but creating a domino effect across the country. If Government continues to sit on the sidelines of the emerging voluntary market, it will be a missed opportunity on a grand scale.

We are not, however, looking to replace the compliance market. In fact, a healthy regulated market is another of the enablers for the expansion of voluntary activity. EU ETS aptly demonstrates that compliance and voluntary markets can work in a complementary manner. It may cover only a limited range of industries, but once it has bedded in, the trading platform created should enable us to understand the true 'price' of carbon for a business – information of great value not only to regulated businesses, but also to the voluntary market. Indeed, the EU ETS has helped create an efficient trading environment applicable to both compliance and voluntary markets, and the scheme allows unregulated businesses to do some forward thinking about the nature of the carbon management obligations they are likely to face in the future – obligations which the voluntary market gives them the opportunity to address. As business experience tells us, businesses that get ahead of the game are far more likely to come out on top in the end.

Developments in one country can, of course, be swamped by developments elsewhere. Fortunately, the globalization of carbon emissions issues can also be seen as an enabler for the expansion of the voluntary market. Though it may be purely pragmatic, the interest of E7 economies like China, India, South Africa, Brazil and Argentina in carbon management could turn the economics of voluntary carbon management on its head. If, for example, China decided to switch from the expense of centralized coal-fired energy and commit to a solar panel for every ten households, the world economics of solar panel usage would change overnight. Apart from driving solutions, the engagement of these economies could also switch the perception of going CarbonNeutral from 'middle-class, developed economy tinkering' to a practical way of addressing the climate crisis that has mass appeal and buy-in.

Although the potential of the voluntary carbon market to exceed the compliance market is anticipated by many market commentators, only action in the next few years will determine whether this materializes. The expansion of the voluntary market is threatened by attitudes which hold that advances in technology may supersede it or that human adaptation to climate change will become the norm. However, the 'move to higher ground' approach is not a practical reality for most people in the world today. Fortunately, support for the voluntary carbon market is gathering pace not only with those businesses seeking to address their carbon liabilities but also within the Government.

The future of the voluntary market

Just as we have looked for signs to prove the existence of global warming itself, so we should look for indicators that the voluntary market is poised to grow and evolve in the next few years. What will tomorrow's telltale signs look like? Here we suggest a few of the developments that could transform the voluntary carbon market in the near future:

- Government endorsement of voluntary action on climate change that encourages it as a valid complement to regulation – rather than ignoring it.
- Evolution of the Carbon Disclosure Project and other such schemes to a level of detail, which allows direct benchmarking of carbon exposure among companies.
- Action on a set of globally accepted standards that enable any reduction activity to be better scoped, implemented and measured (currently there is no way of comparing the performance of one organization against another).
- Use of offsets not just for CarbonNeutral schemes, but to fill gaps between actual reductions and stretching corporate targets (which decouple carbon emissions from commercial growth).
- Convergence between the scientific community and the popular media with respect to the messages on climate change (Al Gore's *An Inconvenient Truth* highlighted that 0 per cent disagreement among scientists translates into 53 per cent uncertainty in the press).
- The setting up of systems that really work when promoting consumer buy-in to corporate carbon management efforts – so people can choose carbon neutral products in the same way that we can choose organic foods and Forestry Stewardship Council-certified furniture.

Perhaps only when we see these signs can we be certain that Einstein's theory of an equal and opposite reaction can be applied accurately to efforts tackling climate change through the voluntary carbon market.

A consultant's perspective on the voluntary carbon market: Does quality matter in environmental commodity markets?

Mark Trexler

Environmental commodity markets are increasingly popular as the world looks for new ways to address increasingly complicated environmental objectives, from biodiversity loss to global warming. With so many environmental problems attributable to market failures of one kind or another, the idea of using markets to counter those problems is an attractive one.

As we develop these new commodities, questions arise about whether or not we should treat them with a hands-off approach and allow consenting parties to structure whatever transaction they feel is appropriate to their needs. In other words, is there something about these commodities that should make third parties particularly interested in their quality, much as they are when things like public health are involved?

Initially I want to explore these questions in the context of GHG credits and RECs. Does quality matter when it comes to GHG credits and RECs? In order to answer this larger question, I pose three related questions:

- Are GHGs and RECs susceptible to market failures that undercut achievement of the objectives around which these two commodities were created?
- Can quality standards be implemented that would prevent such market failures?
- Can market participants implement such quality standards, and will they choose to do so?

Each of these questions can be looked at in turn to explore the larger question of 'does quality matter?'

The greenhouse gas credit market

Are GHG credits susceptible to market failures that undercut achievement of the objectives around which GHG markets were created?

What are the objectives of the GHG market? Presumably, the answer to this question is to achieve climate change mitigation. But mitigating climate change can mean different things to different people. It could mean direct emissions reductions, public education intended to promote climate policy, or deployment of new technologies with climate change benefits over time. An added twist is that not everyone agrees that the goal of GHG emissions trading is climate change mitigation, at least in the near term. Even some environmentalists see the primary purpose of today's nascent GHG markets as being to set the stage for much larger and more material markets in the future, rather than near-term climate change mitigation.

Nevertheless, if we're willing to stipulate that the ultimate goal of GHG markets is climate change mitigation, rather than simply the creation of a new currency per se, it is abundantly obvious that the market is at least susceptible to market failures. With billions of tons of potential CO_2 reductions or sequestration available to the market, many of them being quite 'business as usual,' it is possible to envision an active GHG market in which no climate change mitigation is occurring at all.[3] The potential for market failure is therefore obvious.

Several potential outcomes make the transactions in such a market of interest to market observers beyond the transaction participants:

- The mis-allocation of resources, where market participants are denied the opportunity to purchase the commodity they're really looking for, namely climate change mitigation.
- Making it much more difficult for truly additional GHG projects to find the support they need from GHG credit markets in order to be financially viable.
- Misleading consumers about the nature of what they are buying when, for example, purchasing a carbon neutral product or service.
- Delaying the implementation of more significant emissions reduction policies and measures, based on the argument that large volumes of reductions are occurring through GHG markets.
- An eventual larger loss of faith in market mechanisms as a means of addressing climate change, thus taking a potentially useful policy tool off the table.

These potential outcomes clearly justify a larger societal interest in near-term GHG credit markets. The transactions taking place in GHG markets, including voluntary markets, have the ability to affect our ability to achieve larger climate change mitigation objectives.

Can standards be implemented that would prevent such market failures?

Although GHG standards incorporate many components, the key issue facing any GHG market standard, whether voluntary or mandatory, is additionality. In other words, such market standards must seek to limit participation in GHG commodity markets to transactions that result in 'real' emissions reductions (or sequestration). This is often referred to as the business as usual test, which unfortunately can create substantial misunderstandings among market participants in its own right. A better test is to ask whether the transaction results in emissions reductions (or sequestration) that would not have occurred but for the existence of the GHG market.[4]

Additionality rules, coupled with other criteria relating to the quantification and verification of the reductions covered by a particular transaction, can help prevent the kind of market failures introduced earlier. No additionality rules can be perfect, but it is easy to envision a set of rules that minimizes the number of non-additional reductions making their way into the market (false positives). Such a set of rules, however, could also have the unintended effect of excluding large numbers of truly additional reductions from the market (false negatives). It's a well-understood axiom of statistics that you can't simultaneously minimize for false positives and false negatives. But you can manage for false positives and false negatives in ways that advance the underlying policy objectives of the market.

Can market participants implement such standards, and will they choose to do so?

This is difficult terrain. I don't believe today's GHG markets, whether voluntary or mandatory, effectively prevent the market failures discussed above. Today's markets, and particularly voluntary markets, are not guided by additionality and other rules that ensure that the markets consist primarily of truly additional reductions.

Instead, we see a more aggressive focus on quantification of the emissions reductions. It often seems that quality in GHG markets is seen as synonymous with the level of precision achieved in quantifying the emissions reductions being claimed by a project, or in the elaborate monitoring and verification procedures that are imposed. However, measuring a GHG reduction to within 3 per cent has little to do with the question of whether it was business as usual to begin with. Moreover, imposing onerous monitoring and verification requirements will not make non-additional reductions any more additional.

Why do we see such a focus on the quantification and monitoring of GHG reductions? Imposing meaningful additionality standards inevitably excludes large numbers of potential emissions reductions from the market. Particularly in voluntary markets, there has been little impetus to take the politically difficult step of excluding potential market participants from the market. Focusing on the quantification and verification of reductions makes it appear that the market is quality-oriented, without having to make the difficult decisions implied by an effective additionality policy. Ironically, it can be the non-additional reductions that fare best in the face of high transaction costs associated with quantifying and verifying the reductions, since the underlying reduction may well not have cost anything to begin with. Truly additional reductions, on the other hand, may not be able to absorb those transaction costs, especially if competing with non-additional reductions in the market.

Unfortunately, without effective standards to guide the market, well-meaning buyers and sellers can face enormous difficulties in differentiating between high-quality and low-quality GHG credits. Economic self-interest, at least in the short term, can also push credit buyers to turn a blind eye to credit quality, if that means being able to buy them for a much lower price. If it's difficult to differentiate between high-quality and low-quality credits, and if they serve the buyers' near-term interests equally well, e.g. convincing consumers that they are environmentally sustainable, Gresham's Law tells us that we have a problem.[5]

Now let's turn to RECs.

Renewable energy certificates

Are RECs susceptible to market failures that undercut achievement of the objectives around which REC markets were created?

What are the objectives of REC markets? Presumably, the goal is to promote renewable energy supplies; some market participants might have other objectives, including technology development and climate change mitigation.

The REC market does not face the same possibility of market failures as GHG credit markets, in which billions of 'anyway tons' stand ready to flood the market if the rules of admittance to the market are too loose. In contrast to GHG emissions reductions, it can be argued that any renewable energy is good renewable energy, and that it all helps promote the objective of increasing overall renewable energy utilization.

But there is still the question of what REC markets are intended to accomplish. As with GHG markets, it is presumably to promote renewable energy supplies that otherwise would not have occurred. As with GHG markets, this means that REC purchasers should be able to assume that their purchase of RECs materially contributes to the promotion of renewable energy supplies that otherwise would not have occurred.

Recent history with some categories of RECs throws this assumption into question. REC prices have fallen substantially in recent years. And with national RECs selling for as little as $1/MWh, or 0.1 cents per kWh, we seem to be facing a significant oversupply of RECs as compared to market demand. There are so many new renewable energy facilities being built today (primarily wind facilities) that the number of RECs being generated has grown by leaps and bounds.

Although the demand for RECs has also been growing, it is quite possible that we are buying and selling large quantities of RECs without materially affecting whether more renewable energy facilities are built. In today's market, the question of whether a new wind farm gets built is usually a function of natural gas prices, falling technology prices, and federal tax incentives, rather than being a function of REC sales.

Voluntary GHG markets are being detrimentally affected by today's REC market. With REC prices so low, RECs are being converted to CO_2 and sold as GHG credits. Yet RECs face no additionality test, a key aspect of the GHG market that differentiates it from the REC market to date. Buying non-additional RECs does not reduce one's environmental footprint any more than buying non-additional GHG credits would achieve that goal.

Is it time to declare victory with renewable energy markets, and declare certain types of renewable energy to be business as usual, and thus exclude them from the REC markets much as we try to exclude business as usual reductions from GHG markets? If the potential for market failures in the REC market is modest and likely to be short-lived, such a step may not be appropriate. But the question should be asked if we are to avoid some of the same outcomes potentially facing GHG markets, including:

- The misallocation of resources, where market participants are denied the opportunity to purchase the commodity they are seeking, namely the ability to truly promote new renewable energy supplies.
- Making it much more difficult for truly additional renewable energy projects to find the support they need from REC markets in order to be financially viable.
- Misleading consumers about the nature of what they are buying when, for example, purchasing from a company that claims to have negated the environmental impacts of all of its electricity consumption by purchasing RECs.
- Delaying the implementation of more significant renewable energy policies and measures, based on the argument that RECs already play the needed role.

- An eventual larger loss of faith in market mechanisms as a means of promoting renewable energy, thus taking a potentially useful policy tool off the table.

These potential outcomes clearly justify a larger societal interest in near-term REC markets, even if the sheer magnitude of the problem isn't as large as it is in GHG markets.

Can standards be implemented that would prevent such market failures?

If business-as-usual renewables are a major impediment to REC markets' ability to achieve their underlying objective, the issue is again additionality. The additionality challenge for renewable energy is conceptually identical to the challenge for GHG credits; it should be easier to address, however, given the small number of REC generating technologies as compared to GHG emissions reduction technologies. There is no doubt that additionality rules for renewable energy could prevent the kind of market failures introduced above with respect to RECs.

Can market participants implement such standards, and will they choose to do so?

REC markets have never been subject to additionality testing, and there is little indication that the industry wants to move in that direction.

Some observers argue that today's oversupply of some REC categories is a temporary phenomenon. They argue that the market will absorb the current bubble of excess RECs in the relatively near term, REC prices will rise again, and RECs will be able to play a clearer role in promoting the expansion of renewable energy markets. I don't know if this is true, and I have not seen the question quantitatively analysed in a way that would put market failure concerns to rest. If it were true, then focusing our efforts on building additional demand for voluntary RECs might be a better approach than developing additionality tests for the REC markets. Perhaps there is a mathematical answer to this question, but I don't know what it is.

Conclusions

Quality does matter in the two environmental commodity markets discussed here. These markets were not created simply to create new business opportunities for environmental brokerage houses. The implications of ignoring the quality of what's being traded in these markets could largely undercut the objectives for which the markets were created.

That said, the challenge of developing and implementing quality standards for these markets is considerable. The challenge is not because standards pose overwhelming technical challenges; they don't. But they do pose significant political and policy challenges, since implementing such standards will create much clearer classes of winners and losers than are present in today's markets.

What we need to be cognizant of, however, is that failing to provide for the quality of these markets is more likely than not to mean that everyone loses over the longer term.

An investor's perspective on the voluntary carbon market

David Brand and Marisa Meizlish

Long before there was a Kyoto Protocol or an EU ETS, carbon transactions were occurring. The earliest deals (related to forest conservation and reforestation) began in the late 1980s. Through the 1990s the retail and voluntary markets[6] grew slowly, but certain key developments began to emerge. Companies whose entire business focused on carbon markets were born, including Ecosecurities, Future Forests (now CarbonNeutral), Natsource, CO_2e.com and Evolution Markets. The concept of green power, linked with renewable energy and tree planting programmes as an offset for automobile and air travel emissions began to develop.

While the overall carbon market shuddered for two or three years after the withdrawal of the US from the Kyoto Protocol, the retail and voluntary markets continued to diversify. The Chicago Climate Exchange (CCX) was established in 2003 as the first voluntary carbon credit market. Retail carbon companies proliferated, and there are now more than 30 worldwide. On the demand side, the concept of businesses offsetting some or all of their emissions has become mainstream (e.g. HSBC, Swiss Re, Blackwell Publishing and the World Cup have all offset their emissions). The market is also seeing the emergence of investment funds focused on retail offsets as the focus for some or all their investment programme, such as Cheyne Capital, RNK Capital and Climate Change Capital.

The voluntary market remains somewhat difficult to categorize, and its boundaries are difficult to define, but estimates of the size of this market range from 2 million tons (for specific retail-style carbon offsets) to up to 20 million tons, including a whole range of voluntary offsets, retail offsets, green power programmes, etc. There is no question the market has matured dramatically in the past two years, and most participants feel that the market is growing by 100 per cent or more per annum at this point. Again, there is no formal tracking of the market, but a few studies have been done, and the Ecosystem Marketplace (www.ecosystemmarketplace.com) is increasingly providing centralized information on the sector.

At the tipping point

Organizations ranging in size and character from small NGOs, to events organizers, to major multinational corporations are determining that climate change is an important issue to their customers or stakeholders, and they are taking action to reduce the greenhouse gas emissions associated with their business, event or product. While this may have seemed a quirky thing to do ten years ago, its recent embrace by major mainstream businesses has pushed the voluntary carbon market to a tipping point.

The focus is shifting from the innovators to the laggards, and the question is being asked, 'Why haven't you offset your emissions?'. Companies that have a corporate social responsibility policy or have made statements supporting action on climate change are moving from vague emission reduction commitments to quantifiable reduction targets and how offsets can help achieve them.

The retail side is also growing, although uptake of green or branded carbon products such as green energy, green airline flights and even green automobile loans remain a tiny niche in overall consumer markets. (Often we hear of uptake rates of only 1–4 per cent for products where there is any kind of cost imposed.) However, recent discussions with companies indicate there is some very stretch thinking, with one Australian company recently stating that they would like to see their entire business and all the products they sell becoming carbon neutral by 2015. This kind of thinking would indicate that continued substantial growth is on the horizon in the retail and voluntary market.

A weird and wonderful world

Voluntary and retail carbon offset products include a host of offset types originating from tree planting, forest conservation, industrial gas destruction, energy efficiency programmes, renewable energy credits, changes in animal husbandry or waste management, changes in vehicle fleets and many others.

The retail and voluntary markets are certainly not 'commoditized' at this point, but with the entry into the market of large and reputable buyers, the writing is on the wall for poorly defined or managed offset programmes. Buyers now want standardized offsets with real evidence of additionality and truly independent verification of the offsets. There is also a growing expectation that projects have other social and environmental benefits, such as local employment or biodiversity protection. Many buyers do not necessarily want to buy Kyoto units or other regulated carbon products, largely because they generally are more expensive. Carbon offset suppliers, particularly small projects or types of offsets not well accepted under Kyoto (e.g. forest conservation and reforestation), also find the lower transaction costs and lack of bureaucratic accreditation processes makes the route to market easier with voluntary buyers.

Therefore there is a move afoot to establish standards for voluntary projects, including the Climate, Community and Biodiversity Alliance Standard, the Gold Standard and most recently the Voluntary Carbon Standard being promoted by The Climate Group, the International Emissions Trading Association and the World Economic Forum. To be successful, these standards need to be rigorous yet simple to administer and able to register or accredit projects to create a product that can be sold without a 40-page legal agreement. This maturation process will likely lead to a smaller number of larger carbon offset businesses that can aggregate up projects, manage accreditation and registry processes and create the credibility and verifiability that sophisticated corporate buyers will demand. This process will also likely lead to for-profit companies out-competing the not-for-profit offset providers because they can marshal the resources necessary to support the sophisticated systems and business practices necessary to meet more demanding market standards.

Forest-based offsets

Forestry credits have been a mainstay in the voluntary and retail carbon market from the very earliest deals by AES Corporation and the FACE foundation to protect rainforests in the late 1980s and early 1990s. However, the negotiations around the Kyoto Protocol forestry rules were protracted and strongly influenced by a group of environmental NGOs who sought to minimize the role of forestry in market-based mechanisms. The legacy of this has been a minimal role for forestry under the Kyoto Protocol and its international mechanisms. Nevertheless, other carbon markets are successfully integrating forestry credits, including the NSW Greenhouse Gas Abatement Scheme, the California Climate Action Registry and the CCX.

Forestry credits are very attractive in the retail and voluntary markets. One energy company polled its customers to ask what kind of offsets they would prefer if a green energy product were to be offered to them. Compared against industrial gas destruction, relining pipelines, improving energy efficiency in office buildings and factories and capturing methane from coal mines, forestry was far and away the preferred source of offsets. Companies indicate that using trees and forests for offsets makes sense to consumers, while trying to explain methane destruction or sulfur hexafluoride destruction is confusing and simply does not resonate. As one company executive explained, 'We have been using trees as the imagery of environmental conservation forever, and trying to re-educate consumers to understand methane flaring is too hard.'

However, despite this demand, many of the current initiatives to standardize offsets are falling into a 'Kyoto mindset' on forestry. There are real concerns about permanence and measurement, and these issues are often used to argue that forestry offsets are simply too hard to regulate effectively. For example, a carbon credit from forestry may require an ability to retain carbon stock in forests for 100 years or more. This kind of inter-generational obligation is as compelling as it is daunting. New and innovative approaches are needed to address this, including specialized carbon-pooling vehicles, reinsurance approaches and risk management systems. However, the efforts to exclude forestry may create a self-fulfilling prophecy, with investors shying away from forestry offsets, reducing access to funding and resources dedicated to establishing 'permanence' protocols and measurement standards; the very issues that have been used to keep forestry credits on the sidelines.

Despite this, there is optimism that forestry credits are on a comeback. The COP11 meeting in Montreal in 2005 responded positively to a proposal sponsored by Papua New Guinea and Costa Rica to reopen the discussion on how to accredit avoided deforestation. Recently, the proposal to develop a Voluntary Carbon Standard received substantial resistance when it attempted to marginalize the use of forestry offsets.

Forests provide a natural infrastructure for the planet, regulating the atmosphere, hydrological cycles and much of the biodiversity of life on earth. Forests continue to be lost and degraded, and areas needing re-vegetation or reforestation cannot attract investment. Without price signals for ecosystem services, including carbon sequestration, we are entrenching the status quo of existing economic signals and dooming a significant proportion of our remaining tropical forests in particular to conversion to 'higher uses,' such as palm oil or soybean cultivation.

Towards the future

It appears clear that the voluntary carbon market is growing rapidly, and moving to a new level of standardization and legitimacy. If we reach the tipping point where business begins to move in a substantial way to integrate carbon offsets into its internal management objectives and product offerings, the market could increase by orders of magnitude.

As the voluntary and retail carbon markets go mainstream, we hope that forests and land management are one part of the overall portfolio of offsets. If these markets do reach a level of billions of dollars per annum in turnover, it could make a substantial contribution to forest conservation and reforestation.

An investor's perspective: The challenges ahead for scaling the voluntary carbon market

Alexander Rau

Carbon markets and emissions trading have emerged over the past few years as some of the most promising response options to the growing problem of climate change. While most attention has been focused on the EU ETS and the CDM/JI project markets under the Kyoto Protocol, voluntary carbon markets have been experiencing rapid growth as well. Proactive corporations are beginning to unlock hidden shareholder value by using project-based emissions reductions as a tool complementing internal measures to achieve self-imposed carbon neutrality commitments, or in offering carbon offset products and services in sectors with few short-term technology solutions.

But as with any nascent market there are a number of critical issues as to how the voluntary carbon market will develop over the next few years. These will largely determine what role the market will play in the overall effort to mitigate the climate problem. With a continuation of current practices one might expect the market to grow to tens of millions of tons of CO_2e avoided per year. At this level the voluntary carbon market will be an altruistic attempt at reducing emissions and it will play an important role in educating the public about climate change, but it will not have a meaningful impact on the climate problem.

Conservative estimates from the scientific community suggest that reductions in excess of 500 billion tons of CO_2e are necessary between now and the middle of the century simply to avoid a doubling of the pre-industrial concentration of carbon in the atmosphere. A well-scaled voluntary carbon market could drive reductions in the order of hundreds of millions of tons per year, and thus have a more meaningful impact on shifting the emissions trajectory. The theoretical potential for volumes exceeding this scale exists because of the ability of voluntary markets to target sectors which are beyond the reach of efficient regulation, such as with mobile or diffuse sources in the transportation or building sectors. Even those sectors which are regulated, typically face incremental caps or reduction targets, leaving the majority of emissions untouched. Furthermore, the consumer-facing nature of many voluntary initiatives allows for steady growth subject more to marketing dynamics and intrinsic demand than political dynamics and the volatility of artificial demand.

But in order for the voluntary market to scale to such a meaningful size there are a number of challenges that must be addressed.

Uniform quality standard

First is the need for a consistent set of internationally accepted standards determining which projects create reductions that are truly 'real, quantifiable, and permanent', and the procedures by which those reductions are calculated, monitored, and verified. The current proliferation and simultaneous lack of standards in the voluntary market only undermine confidence and increase the transaction costs of corporate and institutional adopters of market-based voluntary initiatives. The recently launched Voluntary Carbon Standard is a productive first step towards a credible, harmonized standard. Much of its strength lies in its adoption of the experience and intelligence built up over the past years in the international project markets – namely, a large set of project-specific methodologies that have been road tested with billions of dollars of capital across hundreds of projects, and a group of experienced verifiers – without the associated bureaucracy.

Standardized reduction

In order to scale appreciably, the voluntary market also needs to move towards a standardized reduction unit. The fungible nature of the underlying tradable instrument is a key factor contributing to the liquidity of most large financial markets. The current emphasis on linking voluntary carbon credits to particular high-visibility projects may have transitional communication benefits but is not a model that can scale to drive large volumes of emissions reductions or ensure a reliable supply of carbon for voluntary initiatives at realistic costs. Instead, the burden of quality should rest on the standards as discussed above, in which case those reductions verified to have met the standard can effectively be treated as fungible.

Robust market infrastructure

Recognizing that carbon credits from greenhouse gas abatement projects are financial assets, the voluntary market must develop comparable infrastructure to that existing in other asset classes but also tailored to the specific attributes of carbon. The principle components are a custodial registry and retirement platform. Procedures must also be in place to ensure that verified reductions are not double counted, counterparty and settlement risks can be effectively managed, and the retirement of credits can be transparently reported. The Bank of New York has recently launched a custodial registry service for voluntary carbon that addresses these concerns and should give confidence to investors and corporate end-users alike that voluntary carbon assets can be managed in the same reliable manner as are other financial asset classes.

Return on investment

Finally, voluntary carbon must prove a sufficiently attractive investment opportunity in its own right in order to mobilize private capital to finance high-quality greenhouse gas abatement projects in situations where compliance instruments cannot be created. The offset model must also be economically attractive to motivate corporate providers of carbon-intensive products and services to offer transitional offset solutions where there are no short-term technological options or regulatory requirements. Ultimately these corporations are providing customers with an 'environmental service', the revenues from which will spur them to seek innovative ways to develop and market low-carbon/offset products and services.

Addressing these issues will help lay the appropriate conditions for the voluntary carbon market to scale meaningfully. The magnitude of the challenge of stabilizing the atmospheric concentrations of carbon at manageable levels of risk makes it clear that all of the viable response options must be adopted, whether regulatory or voluntary, cap-and-trade or technology-based approaches.

A large and robust voluntary market for project-based emissions has a significant transitional role to play in increasing the flow of funds towards low carbon technologies and shifting the global emissions trajectory.

A buyer's perspective on the voluntary carbon market

Erin Meezan

Increased attention is being paid to voluntary actions to reduce carbon emissions, whether from corporate activities, government commitments or consumers. In 2003, Interface, a leading manufacturer of carpet, took its philosophy and concern over carbon emissions to another level.

Building on its experiences reducing carbon emissions from its manufacturing facilities, corporate cars and employee commuting, Interface launched its first climate neutral product, Cool Carpet^{TM} in 2003. In structuring the Cool Carpet programme, Interface measured the carbon emissions from the entire life cycle of the product and purchased credits to offset the carbon emissions of the carpet. The Cool Carpet programme has made Interface a significant purchaser in the voluntary carbon market and has given the company some perspective on the market's impact to date, as well as some insight into the challenges and opportunities facing it in the future.

Early results

By offering a climate-neutral product, Interface has educated its employees and its customers about climate change issues and solutions. Interface employees, already sensitized to climate issues as a result of the company's sustainability commitment, are now more aware of the climate impacts of their products. By offering a climate-neutral option to customers for a nominal charge, Interface is educating carpet buyers and engaging them to take action to reduce the climate impacts of their purchases.

The Cool Carpet programme has also elevated the issue of climate change in the $23 billion floor coverings industry, where a focus on greener options is increasing every year. Cool Carpet customers, who can calculate the GHG emissions retired from their purchases, are becoming aware of how greener purchasing decisions can benefit corporate environmental commitments. On a broader level, Interface's programme is also providing a model for other manufacturers looking to create climate neutral products and services. Through working groups, case studies, conference presentations and publications, Interface's experiences in the market are providing valuable guidance for companies looking to address climate change.

Aside from its ability to educate and engage, it is clear that the voluntary carbon market also has the potential to help build the capacity of offset providers to respond to consumer preferences. Offset providers supplying the voluntary carbon market today are benefiting from the practical experience of engaging in early transactions and interacting with a small set of customers. By engaging in trades now these providers are learning how to assess transactional costs and risks, while the market is still relatively small, positioning them to respond more efficiently as the market grows. Early participation in these markets will also allow providers to have a better understanding of project costs, standards and certification and consumer preferences. Gaining a better understanding of consumers' desires now will allow providers to anticipate the types of carbon reductions that will need to be supplied to a growing consumer market.

The voluntary market's lack of specific project requirements also allows it to play a valuable role in promoting emerging technologies that avoid or sequester carbon emissions. By not limiting the technological innovation to specific technologies or practices, broad innovations will occur and lead in a direction of lowest cost carbon sequestration. This flexibility also allows for low carbon technologies developed in industrial and commercial sectors to be transferred to other sectors.

And last but not least, the voluntary carbon market is beginning to develop and refine the principles that need to be respected in any future regulatory markets. These principles, which include transparency, real and verifiable carbon reductions, reductions beyond business as usual, transferability and stakeholder engagement, can then provide a basis for a mandatory framework.

Current challenges

The voluntary carbon market has made significant progress over the last year towards a common standard and supporting framework, but the market still lacks universal agreement in key areas. There are multiple protocols available, some proprietary, for what defines a credible carbon offset, and this has hindered the development of a robust voluntary market where there is big potential for one. Another stumbling block has been the diverse manner in which carbon emissions are measured and transferred through the Chicago Climate Exchange and other carbon exchanges.

Increased acceptance in terms of one transparent, unified standard could greatly contribute to the market's size and credibility. A commonly accepted standard for the definition of 'carbon offset' will help the market grow through increased corporate and consumer participation. Consumers want to be assured that they are in fact buying a credible reduction. Purchasing an offset pursuant to one well-defined standard will ease consumer concern and promote purchases. A common standard will also appease corporate customers who have more specific concerns (e.g. the public relations and legal risk associated with buying non-credible emission reductions). Lastly, it will give offset providers certainty and help them avoid having to satisfy multiple protocol requirements, which is costly and time consuming.

Another step forward and benefit to the market could come from an agreed unit for transferring and trading carbon reductions. This would allow for smoother transactions, decreased transactional costs and broader participation of offset providers in the market. As a buyer, I can say with certainty that all of these things would be welcome developments for those interested in investing in the voluntary carbon market.

Future hopes

Few disagree that acceptance of a common standard and adoption of a common tradable unit would have positive growth impacts on the voluntary market. Where there is disagreement however is on the effect of carbon regulation on this market. Many suggest that when carbon is regulated, much of the activity and growth potential for this market will disappear, but I disagree.

To be sure, some corporate strategies will change with regulation and there will be decreased participation in the voluntary markets from some in the corporate sector. However, there will be increased participation from those corporations that will never fall under a cap-and-trade scheme but will adopt climate or environmental goals. There will also be increased participation from product and service providers looking to offer climate-friendly products and services. Their need to offset the life cycle of GHG impacts for these products or services, occurring in the supply chains, will necessitate some form of participation in the voluntary market. Additionally, increased focus on climate will likely mean a more aware citizenry with increased participation in the voluntary market as consumers. We are already seeing the growth of organizations like TerraPass and Sustainable Travel International, offering offsets to consumers to reduce the GHG emissions of their personal commuting and trips.

For all of these reasons, we at Interface are inclined to think that there will be a vibrant voluntary market in 2010. If a cap-and-trade programme has been established in the US, participants in the voluntary market will include consumers using offsets to reduce their personal GHG impacts, entities falling outside of the cap-and-trade regime and others looking to capitalize on the climate business opportunities.

A bank's perspective on the voluntary carbon market: From risk to opportunity – the HSBC carbon neutral experience

Lorna Slade

In 2005, HSBC became the world's first major bank to achieve carbon neutrality.

At the time, Steve Howard, Chief Executive Officer of The Climate Group, summed up the aims of the bank when he said: 'HSBC's decision sets a new benchmark for the financial sector. They will gain a deeper insight into the emerging low carbon economy and be exceptionally well placed to understand the needs of and opportunities for their clients.'

The decision to become carbon neutral took HSBC into uncharted territory, and it admits it came across many challenges that could not have been anticipated during the journey.

The bank's decision to build its expertise in-house, rather than outsource the project to a carbon broker, has endowed it with a deep, first-hand knowledge that it has been able to use for its own and its clients' benefit. Critical to this was the formation of a Carbon Management Task Force, under the sponsorship of the Group Chief Executive, to manage the project. The task force was chaired by Francis Sullivan, HSBC's Adviser on the Environment. Members of this task force were drawn not only from HSBC's corporate real estate and procurement divisions, but also from our energy sector and project finance teams. 'We also made an early decision to involve external experts, recognizing this was all very new to us,' Sullivan said. 'We received excellent support from The Climate Group and ICF Consulting.'

HSBC's Jon Williams, Head of Group Sustainable Development, was part of the team that led the drive to carbon neutrality, and he brings up the question of why HSBC felt the need to become carbon neutral voluntarily. 'Why would any company that doesn't have to comply with Kyoto or the Emissions Trading Scheme (ETS) do what we did? Well, the pressure to reduce our emissions wasn't overt but it did exist, from peers, from shareholders, from the NGOs we work with and from our own staff. But there was no pressure to go one stage further and become carbon neutral. In fact, I think we surprised a number of observers in how far we were prepared to go, and the reason is that we saw climate change as part of a wider look at our environmental footprint.'

After all the measuring, monitoring and buying of 'green' electricity (from renewable sources), the bank realised that it was unrealistic to imagine that it could completely eliminate carbon emissions from its operations. Apart from anything else, 18 per cent of its emissions are produced by business travel, and the bank is growing.

HSBC calculated therefore that it will be left with an annual volume of CO_2 of around 550,000–600,000 tonnes. 'We could have stopped there and said we've done what we can, but we wanted something to give us an understanding of carbon markets and we did not have capability in core global markets business,' Williams said.

To achieve carbon neutrality, HSBC knew that it needed to set some criteria for the offsets it wanted to buy. The criteria were:

1 They had to be *environmentally credible*, that is contribute to sustainable development;
2 *They needed to be additional* in that they genuinely reduced carbon dioxide emissions somewhere else in the world; and
3 Price was also a factor – after all, this was a voluntary initiative – so any offsets had to be *cost-effective* compared to other means to reduce emissions.

Credibility was in fact a key concern and when it began the tender process that would allow it to claim carbon neutrality three months ahead of schedule (for the fourth quarter of 2005 involving 170,000 tonnes of CO_2), the bank tried where possible to purchase offsets from projects directly. 'We felt that really enabled us to get a handle on the underlying sustainability and additionality of each project,' Williams explained.

The choice of whether to buy from the voluntary or more expensive compliance market was, as can be expected of a bank, dictated by economic sense. Said Williams, 'Since there was no requirement on us to enter the compliance market, we could not justify buying from it when we could buy, for example, Gold Standard offsets in the voluntary market at an average of US$4.43.'

The tender process itself was put in motion with a notice on the internet asking for projects from which the bank could purchase offsets. In all, over 100 tenders were received and they included a good range of technologies. HSBC was disappointed, though, not to receive more bids from the developing markets that the bank had prioritized – Brazil, Mexico, China and India.

In retrospect, the time and effort involved in selecting the four projects could have been more cost-effective in that it took one man working full-time for six months to gain three months of carbon neutrality. 'We learned a lot from the experience... and, yes, the procurement exercise was very time consuming and we couldn't repeat it regularly. The aim now is to build it into our core project finance business, to make it an add-on to something we already do and to make it more effective.' As part of that, the Carbon Management Task Force will re-look at the existing projects, and others already financed by HSBC, to try to buy surplus rather than go out to tender again.

Looking back, Jon Williams would turn the emissions monitoring, measurement reporting and purchase of credits into a more seamless process. 'We had a Carbon Management Task Force, which was critical in terms of achieving coordination and which for a one off project is fine, but you can't have that task force reconstructing itself for every project or decision – we need to run it as part of the business.'

The external auditors who verified the emissions might have been involved at an earlier stage in the bank's thinking, speculates Williams. He remembers, 'As it was, Det Norske Veritas had to start us almost from the beginning when they came on board and I think if they had been on board earlier, we might have been able to get the projects verified more quickly. However we shouldn't be too hard on ourselves as it was only through the processes we went through that we came to the decision to get the emissions verified independently.'

HSBC's purchasing department, which was responsible for drawing up supplier contracts with the projects, found itself on an even steeper learning curve than the rest. 'Purchasing had no prior knowledge of carbon markets and I think they found them to be very fragmented and diverse, and the vocabulary was new to them,' Williams said.

But the biggest lesson to emerge from the process, believes Williams, is that the banks own clients might have been a better shopping list to go to: 'We have 125 million customers globally and would have done well to approach those who will be involved in carbon markets or the projects that underpin them,' he says, 'and I'd much rather help an existing client reduce its carbon dioxide footprint, and then pay it for its VERs and bring them into our own carbon neutrality.'

The realization informed the bank's Carbon Finance Strategy, which is very client oriented. 'Clients who are big emitters will be best advised take their projects through the UN CDM process – it will add cost and time but the price premium would be more attractive. For lighter emitters, access to voluntary markets will be more appropriate. We will support both, and we will be absolutely driven by our clients' desires.'

A natural extension of this activity is therefore trading and investing carbon offsets. Jon Williams explains, 'Considering that the bank's emissions are small relative to some of its clients, it might only need one or two projects to achieve carbon neutrality. If one of those projects fails to deliver for some reason, the bank's claim to carbon neutrality could be undermined, so we need to build up a portfolio of around 15 projects to spread the risks. That would involve us in buying more credits than we need, but that's fine because we have clients who are prepared to buy credits from us – we can put them into carbon funds for institutional or private clients to invest in, or we can use them to create a trading position for our global markets business. So actually having a project finance business that's able to originate more carbon than we need, I see as an opportunity not a risk.'

The future of the voluntary market

Jon Williams is very optimistic. 'They are very small at the moment and I don't know that a bank of our size could justify trading solely in the voluntary markets. But I believe they will grow rapidly as more projects opt for the lower cost and shorter process times.'

Before real growth can take place in the voluntary market, three major issues need to be resolved, according to Williams.

'Firstly, there needs to be a single global standard to verify VERs against. The Climate Group has done some good work but there really isn't one out there at the moment.'

'Secondly, there needs to be a standard registry for VERs. CDM credits have a registry under the UN and there is an ETS registry, but within voluntary markets, anyone can produce a VER and claim it to represent carbon emission reductions. Registries also overcome problems of double counting and give confidence to buyers.'

'Thirdly, market transparency needs to improved. There is no standard quoted price for VERs, so it tends to be done by bilateral contract. Any traded market needs free flow of information, including price information on buyers and sellers, and that information just isn't around.'

Where HSBC fits in

Having been such a pioneer, HSBC feels that its role in the scheme of things is assured.

Says Jon Williams: 'We are a financier of projects, including projects to reduce carbon dioxide emissions, so we're right in at the ground floor. And our Carbon Finance strategy means that, rather than just trading VERs, we will actually be helping our clients to generate and sell them.'

'The second area where we fit in,' believes Williams, 'is as mentioned before, as a trader of VERs. The advantage we have is that whenever we finance a project we finance it under the Equator Principles, so the environmental and social impacts in project lending and therefore the credits we buy will have sustainability embedded into them at the project level.'

How the voluntary market relates to the regular market

The two are converging in the sense that much of the framework that is in place in compliance markets is being replicated in voluntary markets, observes Jon Williams. However he does believe that there will always be a price discount in the voluntary market.

In time, Williams feels it is possible that voluntary markets could overtake compliance markets: 'There are a number of initiatives around the world fuelling that – the regional greenhouse gas initiative in the north-east US for example, is an entirely voluntary response by state governments and business to manage down carbon; there are initiatives in California and in Australia – all non-Kyoto markets whose governments are working to reduce carbon – and they could become very large.'

A lot also depends on what happens to the Kyoto protocol, says Williams: 'If it is extended beyond 2012 and a replacement agreement is put in place it could re-balance compliance and voluntary markets. But I do believe that voluntary markets are here to stay and that they will grow and, potentially, overtake compliance markets in time.'

Since becoming carbon neutral, a number of other companies have decided to follow HSBC. 'We see this as a growing trend, for companies, governments and even individuals, as a recognition of the need to collectively combat climate change emerges,' Francis Sullivan said. 'This will add powerful momentum to voluntary markets.'

Notes

1 For comparison, prices in the EU mandatory GHG trading system reached 30 Euros (approximately US$39) per metric ton in its first year of operation.

2 Oregon, Washington and Massachusetts have established GHG requirements for new utilities that can be met by on-site reduction, purchasing offsets or paying into a carbon fund like the Oregon Climate Trust – which later purchases offsets.

3 There are many potential sources of GHG reductions or sequestration that, when traded through GHG markets, do not contribute to climate change mitigation objectives. Imagine if all commercial forestry were given sequestration credits to sell (as if this activity were in fact removing carbon from the atmosphere on net), all nuclear energy installations were given GHG credits to sell (as if such facilities were displacing coal), all ethanol were given GHG credits to sell (as if all use of ethanol is displacing petroleum) and all regulated landfills were given GHG credits to sell

(as if they were avoiding methane emissions). The potential supply of 'reductions,' including those that would have happened even without the intervention of GHG markets, becomes enormous very quickly.

4 For a much more in-depth treatment of additionality, see Trexler, M. C., Broekhoff, D. J., and Kosloff, L. H., 'A Statistically Driven Approach to Offset-Based GHG Additionality Determinations: What Can We Learn?' *Sustainable Dev. Law & Pol'y Journal* 6(2):30–40, Special Edition on Climate Law (Winter 2006).

5 Gresham's Law states that 'Bad money drives out good if they exchange for the same price.' While not a perfect analogy to environmental commodity markets, the point that a low quality commodity can drive a high quality out of the market if we can't differentiate between them is applicable.

6 The voluntary market refers to all purchases of carbon offsets that are undertaken on a voluntary (e.g. not required by law) basis. The retail market is a segment of the voluntary market related to direct purchase by consumers, or purchase of offsets linked with other products such as energy or air travel.

5

A Glance into the Future of the Voluntary Carbon Market

Fifty years ago, the idea that markets would one day be used to protect the environment was little more than science fiction. Thirty years ago, a prediction that markets would one day help control acid rain would have been seen as fanciful. And five years ago, the thought that a European market in GHGs would one day be worth US$8.2 billion would have been considered ridiculous. And yet, all of this has come to pass. Yesterday's fiction is today's reality.

And so it may be with voluntary carbon markets. Today, the thought that there could one day be a large and thriving voluntary market in GHGs – a market where buyers and sellers operate without the threat of regulation – is easily dismissed. And yet, under most people's radar screens, voluntary carbon markets are growing and thriving. As German philosopher Arthur Schopenhauer (1788–1860) once said: 'All truth passes through three stages: First, it is ridiculed; Second, it is violently opposed; and Third, it is accepted as self-evident.'[1]

Though it is not yet self-evident that a voluntary market for GHGs will ever grow large and robust, it is increasingly certain that this market is growing at a rapid clip: from a few million tons three years ago to as much as 20 million tons today (Kenber, 2006). Although we don't currently have the data to prove this growth, the Ecosystem Marketplace will be launching a major data-collection project over the next year to get a handle on the true size of the voluntary carbon market.

A new outlet

In part, the growth of the voluntary carbon market is but a reflection of the meteoric rise of the European and Kyoto carbon markets. As more and more money begins to slosh around these compliance markets, some investors have begun to look for new and undiscovered outlets, for new and different carbon opportunities where the potential for growth is high and the level of competition is low. It should therefore come as no surprise that some are beginning to dip their toes into the growing tide of voluntary carbon transactions. It is still too soon to tell whether or not these bets will pay off. The point, however, is that people and organizations that two years ago would never have paid attention to a voluntary environmental market, are today giving these markets a closer look.

Experienced carbon investors in Europe are not the only parties eying the voluntary carbon market closely. Perhaps the greatest source of interest in the voluntary carbon market has been driven by developments in the US. The last year has seen tremendous movement on the issue of climate change in the US. Climate change has been the subject of cover stories in dozens of major US magazines (*Time, Elle, Wired, Vanity Fair*), as well as several feature films and numerous TV programmes (*An Inconvenient Truth*, CNN, Discovery Channel, CBS, etc.). As a result, the discussion has moved from one that asks 'is climate change real' to one that has begun to seek new ways to address what most now acknowledge is a serious problem. Public opinion, it would seem, is beginning to make the connection between increased storms, heat waves, droughts, and global warming.

Since it looks as though political pressure may soon force the US to do something to address climate change – regardless of what happens in the next Presidential election – there are those who feel that some form of carbon trading in the US cannot be far behind. Indeed, various analysts (Trexler, personal communication, Passero, personal communication, Kenber, personal communication) go further, claiming carbon trading in the US is inevitable and a national programme may even be put in place in the next three to five years.

Already we are seeing small, regional regulated carbon markets emerge in the US (e.g. the Regional Greenhouse Gas Initiative, or RGGI, in the US north-east, trading schemes being discussed in California, Washington, Oregon, and the US Southwest, even a carbon trading deal between California and the UK). Carbon markets, in short, are beginning to sprout in all shapes and forms across the US and, since the country is the world's largest emitter of greenhouse gases, any markets that develop in the US could be relatively large.

Gourmet carbon

Judging from what is happening internationally, and especially in Europe and as a result of the Kyoto Protocol, the future will probably include both large compliance carbon markets and innovative and nimble (though possibly small) voluntary markets. These markets probably will occupy a different niche, will attract different types of buyers and sellers, and will look and feel different. Some of these differences are obvious: lots of bureaucracy, lots of money, and larger players in the regulated market; smaller players, more involved transactions, and more variety in the voluntary market. Some differences, however, are perhaps less obvious: Buyer types and buyer preferences, for instance, will probably be different in each of these markets.

In a market where buyers are only interested in complying with regulations and where credits are completely fungible, buyers will naturally gravitate towards those credits with the least cost. If this means looking towards reducing pollution in large industries and destroying hydrofluorocarbons in China, so be it. The voluntary markets, on the other hand, are likely to be a bit pickier about the carbon they end up buying. Since buyers are in this game voluntarily, they will be looking for the carbon that will give them the biggest political, public relations, and/or 'ethical' bang for their buck. In a way, this is understandable: companies engaging in carbon offsetting for public relations purposes and individuals offsetting their emissions for ethical reasons want to be able to justify their actions easily; they want to feel good about the carbon they are buying. In the case of companies, they also want their carbon purchases to contribute towards risk management. For them, the destruction of exotic gases in large industrial parks in China is less appealing than installing solar panels in Bangladesh, or planting forests somewhere closer to where their customers live.

In other words, whereas the regulated markets are following the age-old evolution of markets towards the commoditization of a good or service – they are creating a form of commodity carbon, where a ton is a ton is a ton, no matter the source – a portion of the voluntary markets appears to be gravitating towards a value-added model; one that seeks to provide what we might call 'gourmet carbon,' where the provenance and feel-good attributes of the carbon play an increasingly important role.

The commodity carbon vs. gourmet carbon divide has implications for the price elasticity of carbon offsets in the two markets. Where carbon is simply a commodity, prices will be driven to their lowest possible level, they will be determined largely by the costs of production and their ability to provide compliance (i.e. meet the standards established by regulators), and will tend to deviate less from some fixed point of reference (such as the price of carbon on a given exchange). By contrast, where carbon is bought for its various attributes, where price is not the only factor, and where people have their heart set on projects that simply feel good, the price will probably fluctuate across a larger band, based largely on budgets, on consumer preference, and on the supply of similar projects available to the market. As the market becomes more standardized, and as voluntary carbon commodities such as the Voluntary Carbon Unit (VCU) enter the market, this might change slightly, but a tension between industrial buyers and speculators who want a fungible commodity and other buyers whose main interest is the overall feel of the projects they are funding, likely will remain. This would seem to suggest that, even with the advent of standardization schemes, there will always be a market for carbon with additional certifications and assurances of provenance – a kind of *Appellation d'Origine Contrôlée* in the voluntary market.

The broad spectrum

Pushed and pulled by different buyers with different needs, the voluntary market may one day split itself into two main segments: one large, more commoditized market aimed at speculators and large companies interested in offering standardized climate neutrality with their products; and one smaller, more idiosyncratic market aimed at individuals and companies interested in specific types of offset projects (e.g. trees, community development, and/or renewable energy). In the first market, there will be a kind of currency (like the VCU or VER) that gets traded and ensures quality, helps provide risk management, and generates political cover. In the second market, offset projects will be differentiated by type, by provenance, and by their provision of 'co-benefits' to the environment or to local communities.

If the buyers end up being mostly large corporations wanting to brand their products as carbon neutral, then standardization of the market (with certifications similar to the Green-e label currently being used for renewable energy) will become increasingly likely. If, however, the buyers are overwhelmingly individuals and corporations simply wishing to give themselves a green image, then the market will tend to focus mostly on value added and will follow the gourmet carbon approach – where carbon comes in many different looks and flavours. Again, it may not be an either/or scenario. It is quite possible – maybe even probable – that both types of buyer will co-exist within one market. In that case, we could imagine a situation where carbon is certified to a certain level, a floor, and then has additional certifications or branding based on its various co-benefits (e.g. is it good for communities, for biodiversity, does it come from Mexico, China, the US, etc.).

In a way, this means that parts of the voluntary carbon market will come to resemble the compliance carbon market, and parts will diverge significantly. Perhaps we should look at them as part of a broader spectrum of carbon markets ranging from compliance commoditized markets, through voluntary commoditized markets, all the way to voluntary gourmet markets.

Unanswered questions

At the same time that interest is growing in the broad spectrum of carbon markets, initiatives designed to standardize and certify voluntary carbon offsets are beginning to take shape, suggesting that a self-reinforcing cycle of growth, attention, and interest in voluntary carbon has started to move.

And yet, many questions remain. Even though the voluntary carbon markets may be bigger – and more profitable – than anyone would have imagined five years ago, it is also becoming clear that these markets are not without complications, and that further growth will not be possible unless certain fundamental issues are addressed.

How will the voluntary market interact with the regulated carbon markets and with other existing environmental markets? Will the demand for voluntary carbon prove sustainable, and if so, what will drive it? Will voluntary carbon offsets be standardized in ways that will help the market grow? And, if so, will it be done in ways that negate some of the voluntary market's greatest strengths (innovation, flexibility and the ability to include communities in developing countries)? Last but certainly not least, will the market deliver on its promise to help tackle climate change?

This publication has sought to ask all of these questions and to weigh answers to some of them, but we readily acknowledge that definitive answers are not possible yet because they depend on political choices that have yet to be made, and on the behaviour of thousands of individual and corporate buyers.

Moving toward answers

What we can already say is that the voluntary carbon market is rapidly becoming an interesting public relations and risk-management option for companies, at the same time that it helps involve and educate consumers about the importance of combating climate change. Already, these markets are providing the sort of innovation and flexibility that is simply not possible via the regulated markets. They are allowing more types of people to participate in carbon trading, and they are allowing more types of offsets to be sold.

On the issue of voluntary vs. regulatory, we think that the voluntary carbon market will ultimately find a way to co-exist with regulated carbon markets. We think this co-existence can and should be beneficial to all concerned; with the voluntary markets helping to fill gaps in the regulated market. And we think voluntary markets should not be seen as alternatives to regulated markets, but rather as a supplements; supplements that can help educate and engage broad sectors of society in the fight against climate change, and that can help provide the sort of flexibility, inclusiveness, and innovation that will become increasingly necessary if we are to address climate change. The question of voluntary vs. regulatory is, therefore, nothing but a false dichotomy.

Where the issue of voluntary vs. regulatory markets does get interesting, however, is in the interaction between voluntary carbon markets and regulatory (as well as voluntary) markets for renewable energy certificates, or RECs. We have devoted an entire chapter of this book to this issue, because we see it as a potential source of much pain and many problems on both sides. Currently, the market for RECs and the fledgling markets for carbon (at least in the US) have been somewhat conflated. On the one side, both buyers and sellers of RECs advertise and justify their activities in terms of carbon emissions reductions. On the other, sellers of voluntary carbon are often selling RECs as a substitute for CO_2 emissions reductions. So what happens once there is a more robust market for carbon? Does a large part of the market for RECs get subsumed into the carbon market? Does this kill the REC market, or does it just force it to change shape?

Niels Bohr, the Nobel-prize winning physicist is said to have quipped: 'Prediction is very difficult, especially if it's about the future.'[2] This caveat not withstanding, our prediction is that parts of the REC market will be subsumed into the carbon markets, and parts will remain outside it. The parts that will most likely remain impervious to the carbon markets will probably be the regulated REC markets, with much of the voluntary REC market using the carbon markets as a convenient outlet.

On the issue of demand, we believe that there will be two distinct (and somewhat different) sources of demand for voluntary carbon. One source will come from individuals and institutions interested in playing a role in addressing climate change. The size of this particular customer base is currently hard to gauge, since it will depend to a large extent on how the climate change problem continues to be perceived by the general public. It will also depend somewhat on whether or not people feel governments are doing enough to address the problem. The second source of demand is likely to be corporations and institutions that feel compelled – for a variety of reasons – to go beyond regulation to address climate change. Here again, the size of this market will depend on public opinion and the ultimate scope of government regulation. In other words, if companies feel that their consumers expect them to become climate neutral, if there appears to be a preference in the market (or some other business case) for climate neutrality, then companies will be in the market for offsets. The scope of regulation is important here, too, because if climate regulation is believed to be exceedingly strict, or if it is seen by all as being sufficient to address the perceived problem, then there will be little incentive to participate in a voluntary market.

Additionally, it is important to note that these two potential sources of demand will likely have two very different approaches towards buying carbon: Large buyers will want to minimize transaction costs and ensure adequate levels of risk management. For this reason they are likely to push for standardization and a further commoditization of voluntary carbon. This could lead to rapid growth (in terms of volume) of the market, but it could, at the same time, mean more money being spent on certification and verification, and less money making it down to the ultimate producer of the carbon. This is a trend we have seen with many other commodities: from coffee and sugar, to corn and pork bellies.

Smaller individual buyers, on the other hand, will have a different approach towards buying carbon. They will be in the market for gourmet carbon, carbon that has various other beneficial qualities, whether they be environmental, social, or otherwise. In this market, the price will depend on the qualities of the carbon being offered and sellers will seek to 'brand', 'certify', or otherwise make the carbon they have offer palatable to consumers.

On the issue of standardization, we believe that large parts of the voluntary carbon market will become increasingly standardized, but we hope this standardization is done in such a way that it does not effectively prevent small producers in developing countries from entering the market. We hope that the search for confidence, certainty, and fungibility does not take away from the flexibility, innovation, and inclusiveness that is such a hallmark of the voluntary carbon market. To do this, we feel it is important for those developing standards for voluntary carbon not to be unnecessarily restrictive in the types of carbon offsets that can be considered, and that they come up with inexpensive and cost-effective ways of ensuring and verifying additionality; ways that don't impose too onerous a cost on carbon producers.

In all likelihood, this will require the creation and use of in-country certifiers and verifiers.

This is perhaps an interesting role for philanthropic donors to play: financing the training and creation of in-country carbon certifiers, or perhaps the creation of a 'certifier of certifiers' approach such as that undertaken via the Forest Stewardship Council. Either way, this is an issue that needs to be quickly resolved. For it would be a shame if the old chestnut of the agricultural community – that there is money to made in food, just not from growing it – were to one day apply to carbon providers in developing countries.

And, finally, on the issue of quality, we believe this issue will be an ongoing and never-ending battle for the voluntary carbon markets, and that the pendulum will forever swing from the desire for ever-greater assurances of the quality of offsets (and therefore rigour in the certification) on the one side, all the way to the desire for lower transaction costs, more innovation, and inclusiveness (and therefore simpler certification mechanisms) on the other. Currently the market is experiencing a strong push towards greater rigour and greater assurances of product quality. This is as it should be. For too long the market has operated with little or no emphasis on quality; a trend that could, if taken too far, seriously dampen (if not quell) the market's potential for growth.

Overall, however, we would argue that the future of voluntary carbon markets looks bright. As storms – literal, figurative, and political – batter the concept of climate change into the public consciousness, companies, governments, and concerned citizens will begin to look for simple and creative solutions to this global problem. In doing so, they will inevitably turn to markets, one of the most cost-effective and proven tools for reducing emissions of an atmospheric pollutant.

Even if the voluntary carbon market does not mature into a truly robust market, it will remain a source of innovation, inspiration, and education. The market will also continue to serve as an interesting barometer of public opinion for businesses weighing options for branding and risk-management.

So if the massive clouds that made up the numerous hurricanes that struck around the world in 2004 and 2005 had a silver lining, it was this: they have helped breathe new life into a global market in voluntary carbon emissions reductions that, one way or another, will play an important role in our efforts to stem climate change for years to come.

Notes

1 www.quotationspage.com/quote/25832.html
2 http://en.wikiquote.org/wiki/Niels_Bohr

References

Kenber, M. (2006) Presentation at GreenT Forum: Raising the Bar for Voluntary Environmental Credit Markets. New York, 2–3 May, 2006.

Appendix 1

Offset Project Types

A major variation between carbon credits is the origin of the offset. As noted in Chapter two, carbon credits can be generated via allowance-based or project-based emissions reductions (offsets). With the exception of CCX credits or those retired from the regulatory market, all credits in the voluntary sector originate from offset projects. Offset projects can be categorized into two main categories: those reducing GHG emissions at the source and those that reduce GHG levels in the atmosphere by sequestration. Commonly used emission reduction and sequestration projects can then be further categorized, as illustrated in Figure A.1. There are other means of generating carbon credits than listed in this section. For example, developing technologies, such as the multiple forms of oceanic and geographic sequestration that may lead to GHG sequestration and carbon credits in the future are not discussed. Instead this section focuses on the most widely used sources of offset credits in the voluntary market.

The following section outlines the attributes, disadvantages and advantages of these various project types. It is important to note that many of the different advantages and disadvantages are project and situation specific. The goal of this section is to generalize for the purpose of comparison.

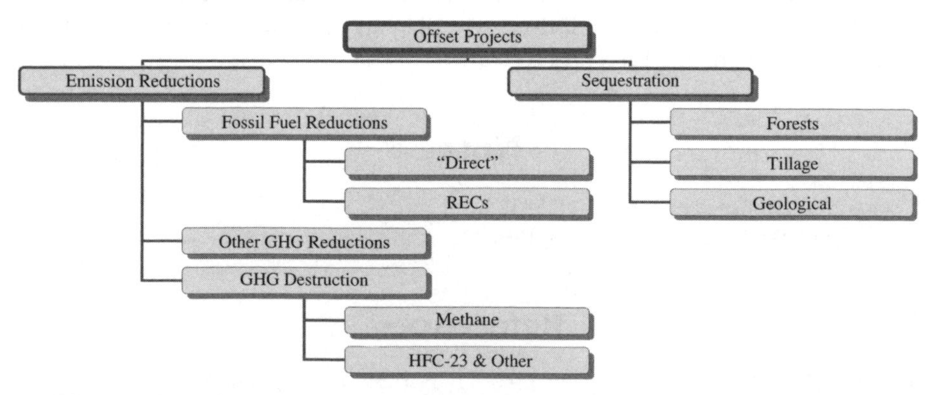

Figure A.1 *Commonly used emission reduction and sequestration projects*

Emissions reductions projects

Projects in the GHG emissions reduction category can be classified, by type of gas reduced or destroyed, into two categories: fossil fuel emission reduction projects and GHG destruction projects.

Fossil fuel emission reduction projects

The burning of fossil fuels is the leading cause of climate change. Hence, reducing the use of fossil fuels is a critical piece of GHG mitigation. As described in Chapter 3, projects may reduce the use of fossil fuel *directly* or *indirectly*. Projects reducing emissions directly generate CO_2 emission reductions through activities such energy efficiency projects, fuel switches, power plant upgrades, and off-grid renewable energy projects, such as small hydro, wind, and biomass. For example, Mercy Corps sells offsets generated by a Climate Trust truck stop electrification project in Oregon (truckers 'plug in' rather than run their engines to generate music, light and heat in their vehicles). The Solar Electric Light Fund (SELF) sells solar energy projects that replace diesel generators in countries such as Nigeria. My Climate, meanwhile, sells credits from replacing coal with biomass burning. Credits generated from grid-connected renewable energy projects, such as wind farms, create RECs, which are often considered indirect emissions reductions.

A major advantage of fossil fuel reduction projects is the numerous potential environmental and human health co-benefits. Reducing fossil fuel combustion also reduces other air pollutants like carbon monoxide, nitrous oxide (another GHG), nitrogen dioxide, particulate matter, and sulfur dioxide, which have negative effects on human health and the environment. Reducing fossil fuel use may also lead to national security benefits from decreasing dependence on fossil fuels, incentives for improving and transferring renewable energy technology, and job creation. Small off-grid renewable energy projects may lead to reduced deforestation by relieving pressure on wood fuel sources. Direct reductions, such as those from energy efficiency projects often result in long-term cost savings,

These benefits not withstanding, generating credits via fossil fuel reductions can be relatively inefficient from a return on investment point of view. Flaring methane, a gas with a global warming potential (GWP) 23 times that of CO_2 over a hundred year period, or destroying HFC-23 (with a GWP 11,700 times that of CO_2) over a hundred year period, for instance, will generate far more credits per dollar invested (www.ipcc.ch/pub/reports.htm/). See Chapter 3 for more information on the advantages and disadvantages of direct versus indirect (REC) credits.

Other GHG emission reduction projects

Under the CDM and within the voluntary market there are also some incentives for the reduction of other Kyoto GHGs, such as perfluorocarbon (PFC), an industrial gas produced in the manufacture of semi-conductors, and sulfur hexafluoride (SF_6) a gas used for insulation and in aluminum and electronics manufacturing. With a 100 year GWP of 23,900, IPCC rates SF_6 as the most potent greenhouse gas. Because these gases have such high GWP, reducing their emissions is often considered important 'low hanging fruit'. PFC and SF_6 reductions also produce credits on the CCX market. However research for this book found no retail offset providers selling credits from these emissions reductions.

GHG destruction projects

Unlike CO_2 emissions, emissions from gases such as methane can be captured and flared. Methane projects are the most common project in the voluntary market, especially in the retail market. However, credits from the destruction of other potent GHGs such as hydrofluorocarbons (HFCs) are also available.

Methane projects

Currently, both CERs and VERs have been produced by capturing and flaring methane from landfills, livestock manure 'lagoons', and coal mines. Methane capture offset projects are extremely popular due to methane's high GWP and because methane flaring also may be used to generate renewable energy for on- or off-grid purposes. Hence, in some areas of the world, a methane project may create two sets of potential offsets, one from the direct methane destruction and the other from RECs. The energy generated from methane projects can also increase the project return on investment to the extent that carbon financing may or may not be a necessary incentive for project creation.

The different types of methane projects have some unique advantages, disadvantages, and co-benefits.

Livestock

In large-scale livestock, especially hog and dairy farming, animal manure is liquefied and stored in large, often open lagoons. These lagoons emit strong odours, methane, and ammonia, a precursor to the air pollutant PM10 (Kunz, 2006). The manure is often spread on fields for fertilizer, resulting in emissions of carbon dioxide and nitrous oxide, as well as excessive nutrient discharges in local water (Amey, 2005). Techniques for recovery include a range of anaerobic digesters in covered lagoons (www.methanetomarkets.org/). Methane is flared and then sometimes used by the farmer to help fuel operations.

The numerous co-benefits resulting from this type of operation are a comparative advantage with other methane projects (Barbour, 2006). A major social co-benefit is reduced odour. Environmental benefits include reduced ammonia, and a reduced risk of lagoons overflowing manure into local water supplies. If the manure is spread on fields post methane removal, another benefit of the methane trapping process is further-reduced groundwater contamination (Kunz, 2006).

Landfills

According to the Methane to Markets Partnership, a voluntary international partnership to advance the recovery and use of methane, landfills account for 13 per cent of global methane emissions (www.methanetomarkets.org/). The US and Europe often require that large landfills be covered and the methane emissions flared. Landfills in many developing countries, however, are generally exempt from such regulation. Decomposing matter emits landfill gas (LFG), which is about 50 per cent methane, and about 50 per cent CO_2. The methane, if trapped and flared, can be a source of energy. The co-benefits from landfill projects in general can be considered less substantial than benefits from livestock, but include some level of reduced odour and often a reduced likelihood of pollutants leaching into groundwater (www.carbonfinance.org/).

Coal mines

Globally, coal mining accounts for 8 per cent of total methane emissions resulting from human activities. Both active and abandoned mines release methane (methanetomarkets.org/). Due to the potential for built-up methane to cause explosions, laws require the removal of methane from active mines around the world. The cheapest method for removing methane from mines is to release it into the air through vents. Alternatively, coal mine methane can be trapped and flared to generate electricity (www.carbonfinance.org/). Compared to landfill and livestock operations, the co-benefits from this process are fairly minimal (Kunz, 2006), but methane capture projects may lead to updated or beyond safety mechanisms, especially in developing countries.

Industrial GHG destruction

Like methane, trifluoromethane (HFC-23) and nitrous oxide (N_2O) are Kyoto GHGs that can be both reduced or destroyed. HFCs are often used to replace the internationally regulated ozone-depleting greenhouse gases chlorofluorocarbons (CFCs) in many applications, such as refrigeration. While HFCs are not ozone depleting and have generally lower GWP than CFC, they are still powerful GHGs, with 100-year GWPs of between 140 and 11,700 (www.epa.gov/highgwp/scientific.html/). N_2O is also a powerful greenhouse gas with a global warming potential 320 times higher than CO_2. Major sources of N_2O include agricultural activities, fossil fuel combustion, nitric acid production, and solid waste burning (www.yosemite.epa.gov/oar/globalwarming.nsf/content/emissions.html/).

Emissions reductions of both these gases can produce credits on the CCX market. There is also approved methodology for the destruction of these gases under the CDM. HFC-23 destruction is the most common sources of offset credits from this category of projects. However, sales of credits from HFC-23 remain particularly rare in the retail market. Research for this book found only one supplier, Natsource, selling credits from Dupont's destruction of HFC-23. This is potentially due to two issues. First only a few companies in the world, such as DuPont, create HFC-23. Second destruction of these gases boasts few to no social or environmental co-benefits. Wiley Barbour of Environmental Resources Trust (ERT) notes, however, that HFC-23 destruction projects could help pull major chemical companies into the global carbon market.

Sequestration projects

The projects listed above avoid the release of a variety of GHG emissions into the air. In contrast, sequestration projects pull carbon dioxide out of the air. Sequestration-based projects aim to increase the number and productivity of natural carbon sinks in forests, oceans and agricultural soils. Within the sinks category, two types of projects currently source credits into the voluntary market: land use projects (forestry and no-till farming) and geological sequestration projects. Land use projects, referred to as Land Use, Land Use Change, and Forestry (LULUCF) projects under the Kyoto protocol, can also be considered 'biological' projects, and geological sequestration 'technology' projects. Because of the relatively new technology used in geological sequestration, land use projects, especially forestry projects are far more common sources of carbon credits in the voluntary market.

Land use projects

The advantages and disadvantages of land-based projects are hotly debated in both the regulatory and voluntary carbon markets. For example, the CDM board has approved some forestry mechanisms but has not yet approved any tillage projects. Proponents of land-based projects note that, while sequestration projects are not permanent, they immediately slow down the amount of GHG entering the atmosphere and could help mitigate climate change during a critical period while other technologies are developed. Describing the importance of using land-based projects, Patrick Zimmerman, Director of the Institute of Atmospheric Sciences at the South Dakota School of Mines and Technology summarizes his view of carbon land-based sequestration by asking and answering two questions. 'Is it permanent?, no. Is it important? You bet it's important' (Zimmerman, 2006).

Forestry projects

Agroforestry, afforestation (planting trees on areas with no previous cover), reforestation, and forest conservation projects are currently the most common type of sequestration project in the voluntary carbon market. An estimated 20–25 per cent of anthropogenic GHGs in the atmosphere results from deforestation. Hence, projects that lead to more global forest cover clearly play a role in GHG mitigation.

Proponents of forestry in the voluntary market cite not only their clear role in sequestering CO_2, but also the numerous co-benefits of forestry projects. Well-managed forestry projects contribute to biological diversity, increased forest productivity, reduced erosion, hydrological regulation, and economic development. Because most consumers have been exposed to the carbon cycle at some point in their education, forestry offsets may also be the easiest type of sequestration offsets for consumers to understand. Denis Slieker, director of Netherlands-based offset provider Business for Climate, notes that 'One reason people want forests is because [they are] tangible.... It also has an emotional aspect. It not only helps the climate, it's also a home for the animals and community development.' (Biello, 2006)

Erica Graetz, programme and operations manager for The Climate Trust, observes, 'There are a lot of co-benefits to using carbon money to fund reforestation as far as air, biodiversity and water quality goes but there's also a lot of risk associated with it.' The most major risk is the question of permanence. 'You cannot guarantee that the trees will still be there in 40 years if there's a forest fire or logging,' (Biello, 2006) notes MyClimate's Corinne Moser. Such uncertainty becomes particularly important for carbon accounting. Forestry projects usually use 70–100 year 'ex-ante' accounting. Financing the initial cost of a forestry project is risky, since the offsets may not occur (Burnett, 2006). If forests are logged, carbon storage depends partially on the end use of the trees. Forestry sinks also give rise to questions about leakage. Specifically, critics of forestry projects point out that it is difficult to guarantee that transforming agricultural land into forest in one area, will not drive clear-cutting to provide land for farming somewhere else.

Moreover, recent studies have highlighted new questions about the nutrient cycle of forests. For example, a recent study in *Nature* suggested that plants may actually contribute to global methane emissions. However, Thomas Rockman, co-author of the original study, notes, 'Climatic benefits gained through carbon sequestration by reforestation far exceed the relatively small negative effect (of methane production)' (Burnett, 2006). While some critics cite such uncertainty as a strike against forestry, proponents of forestry projects hold that they present an important opportunity for further scientific understanding of forests' role in climate regulation (Bayon, 2005).

Last but not least, large monoculture forestry projects that sequester CO_2 may not include the co-benefits provided by indigenous forests. Monocrop plantations, especially those in the tropics that can support fast growing trees such as Klinki, are attractive for carbon offset projects because they generate emissions reductions relatively cost-effectively and quickly. However, critics note that many of these projects contribute little to biodiversity conservation, and may even reduce water supplies or have negative social impacts. Brett Orlando, climate change advisor at the IUCN-World Conservation Union in Switzerland, summarizes: 'The question is, will sequestration be maximized at the expense of other social and environmental objectives? Carbon sequestration is just one of the services that forests provide' (Nicholls, 2005).

Tillage sequestration projects

Carbon offsets from soil sequestration are far less common than forestry credits in the carbon market, but the CCX recently included soil sequestration due to low-till and no-till farming, along with grass planting, on their list of verified offset projects. And in the US, federal agencies have prepared an extensive methodology for calculating emissions reductions projects on agricultural lands. In no-till farming, crop residues are left in the fields to increase the amount of carbon stored in soils. Co-benefits can include reduced soil erosion, emissions reductions from farm equipment and increased soil organic material (www.epa.gov/sequestration/ag.html/). Some critics of agricultural sequestration note that such projects generally would not pass a 'financial' additionality test because they do not capture enough carbon to provide the financial incentive necessary to change farming practices. More importantly, projects may have even less permanency than forestry projects. The carbon sequestered can be quickly lost in a season when a farmer changes tilling practices (Barbour, 2006).

Proponents of obtaining offsets from tillage counter that it is important to send the price signal to farmers that no/low-till farming is desirable. Like forests, they say, the soil represents a major carbon sink; deep ploughing techniques can be equated to 'mining the soil for carbon' (Barbour, 2006).

Geological sequestration: enhanced oil recovery

A variety of geological and oceanic sequestration technologies are now evolving. This section discusses only one type of such sequestration: enhanced oil recovery. Credits from this type of sequestration are relatively rare in the voluntary market. For example in the retail market, research for this book found only one organization, Blue Source in partnership with Natsource, selling credits from capturing waste CO_2 to inject into fields to access hard-to-reach oil reserves. IPCC estimated in 2005 that more than 2,000GtCO_2 could be stored in geological formations (IPCC, 2005). This process also leads to domestically produced oil and may substitute for an alternative process of purposefully mining CO_2 to recover oil. That said, critics cite numerous disadvantages associated with this technology when it comes to creating carbon credits for the voluntary market. For example, since this type of sequestration may be profitable without carbon finance, it likely fails the investment additionality test. Second, the process enables the US 'addiction to fossil fuel' and there are few environmental or social benefits associated with the effort.

References

Amey, A. (2005) 'Manure Power: Capitalizing on Manure', www.climatechangecentral.com/

Barbour, W. Interviewed by Katherine Hamilton May 2006

Bayon, R. (2005) 'Carbon Sinks and Emissions Trading: Room For Optimism', *The Ecosystem Marketplace,* www.ecosystemmarketplace.com/
Biello, D. (2005) 'Speaking For the Trees', *The Ecosystem Marketplace,* www.ecosystemmarketplace.com/
Burnett, M. (2006) 'Buying Greenhouse Gas Offsets: Choosing Between Emissions Reduction Projects and Carbon Sequestration Projects'
IPCC (Intergovernmental Panel on Climate Change) (2005) Metz, B *et al.* (eds), *Carbon Dioxide Capture and Storage,* Cambridge, Cambridge University Press
IPCC (2005) 'Second Assessment Report', www.ipcc.ch/pub/reports.htm/
Kunz, J. Interviewed by Katherine Hamilton May 2006
Nicholls, M. (2005) 'Credits for Sinks', *The Ecosystem Marketplace,* www.ecosystemmarketplace.com/
Trexler, M. Interviewed by Katherine Hamilton May 2006
Zimmerman, P. (2006) 'The Quality Challenge: Are All Credits Created Equal?' Speech given at *The Green-T Forum: Raising the Bar for Voluntary Environmental Credit Markets,* New York City

Websites

Carbon Finance website: www.carbonfinance.org/
EPA High Global Warming Potential Gases websites: www.epa.gov/highgwp/scientific.html/
www.yosemite.epa.gov/oar/globalwarming.nsf/content/emissions.html/
EPA Carbon Sequestration website: www.epa.gov/sequestration/ag.html/
Methane to Markets website: www.methanetomarkets.org/

Appendix 2

Examples of Project Verifiers

There are hundreds of project verifiers in the voluntary market. Some organizations prefer to use local verifiers. Others have lists of accredited verifiers. For example, the CCB Standards use any company already accredited by CDM or Forest Stewardship Council. Below is a partial list of verifiers.

Table A2.1

Name	***Corporate headquarters***	***Ex. types of projects***	***Ex. accreditation***
AENOR – Spanish Association for Standardisation and Certification www.aenor.es/	Madrid, Spain (Multi-national)	A wide variety: forestry, landfill/ livestock methane, fuel switching, etc.	CDM accredited
Bureau Veritas Quality International Holding S.A. (BVQI Holding S.A.) www.bvqina.com	London, England (Multi-national)	A wide variety: forestry, landfill/ livestock methane, fuel switching, etc.	California Climate Action Registry accredited, CDM accredited, CCX accredited
Det Norske Veritas (DNV) www.dnv.com/	Oslo, Norway (Multi-national)	A wide variety: forestry, landfill/ livestock methane, fuel switching, etc.	California Climate Action Registry accredited, CDM accredited, CCX accredited
ENSR Corporation www.ensr.aecom.com/	Massachusetts, US (Multi-national)	Corp GHG inventories	California Climate Action Registry accredited

Table A2.1 *Continued*

Name	***Corporate headquarters***	***Ex. types of projects***	***Ex. clients/ ex. credited***
First Environment Inc. http://firstenvironment.com/	New Jersey, US (Multi-national)	Landfill methane	California Climate Action Registry accredited
G.N. Richardson & Associates www.gnra.com/	North Carolina, US	Landfill methane	CCX accredited
ICF Consulting www.icfi.com	Virginia, US (Multi-national)	Energy efficiency	California Climate Action Registry accredited, CCX accredited
SES Inc. www.ses-corp.com/	Kansas, US	Livestock methane, agricultural practices	CCX accredited
SGS www.sgs.com/	Geneva, Switzerland (Multi-national)	A wide variety of project types	California Climate Action Registry accredited, CDM accredited, CCX accredited
TUV Industrie Service GmbH TUV SUD GRUPPE (TUV Industrie Service GmbH TUV) www.tuev-sued.de/en	Cologne, Germany (Multi-national)	Forestry	California Climate Action Registry accredited, CDM accredited
TÜV NORD CERT www.tuev-nord-cert.de/english/	Germany (multiple cities) (Multi-national)	A wide variety: forestry, landfill/livestock methane, fuel switching, etc.	CDM accredited
Winrock International www.winrock.org	Arkansas, US (Multi-national)	Forestry	The Conservation Fund, Conservation International

Appendix 3
Standards

This section outlines the major carbon offset, or institutional 'carbon neutral' standards around the world and then compares key differences between them. These standards can be separated into several categories: accounting protocols, programmes that implement such protocols and certify companies or products, and those that certify offset projects and carbon credits. These various standards do not fit neatly into such categories, but rather have a range of characteristics. It is important to note that CCX has its own standards and hence represents a certification system within the CCX market. CCX standards are compared with others, but not discussed again in this section.

The WRI/WBCSD GHG Protocol

The Greenhouse Gas Protocol Initiative is a multi-stakeholder partnership launched in 1998 by the World Resource Institute (WRI) and World Business Council for Sustainable Development (WBCSD) with the goal of 'harmonizing GHG accounting and reporting standards internationally to ensure that different trading schemes and other climate related initiatives adopt consistent approaches to GHG accounting.' (www.ghgprotocol.org/). The GHG Protocol Initiative consists of two different sets of standards. The Corporate GHG Reporting Standard was designed to help organizations identify, calculate and report GHG emissions. The Project GHG Accounting and Reporting Standard is a general guide for offset projects that was created with the aim of developing project accounting and reporting standards.

Unlike the other standards described in this section the WRI/WBCSD GHG Protocol is currently an accounting guide that does not certify offsets or organizations. However, the Protocol now plays a major role in setting guidelines for GHG reporting. Numerous institutions, such as Chicago Climate Exchange and US EPA Climate Leaders have utilized the protocol guide in creating their own standards or certification programmes.

ISO 14064

The ISO 14064 standard is a global GHG accounting, reporting and verification standard, which is part of the international ISO 14000 'family' of standards, which includes ISO14001, a well known environmental management system, 'implemented by more than 90,000 organizations in 127 countries'. The goal of the standard is, 'to provide a set of unambiguous and verifiable requirements or specifications to support organizations and proponents of GHG emissions reductions projects.' (Kook Weng and Boehmer, 2006). Like all ISO programmes, ISO 14064 is a 'process-based' certification system, rather than a means of verifying a specific end product. For example, ISO does not require use of specific additionality tests, but rather ISO guidelines state that organizations can 'select establish, justify and apply criteria and procedures for demonstrating that the project results in GHG emissions reductions or removal enhancements that are additional to that what would occur in a baseline scenario.' (Boehmer, 2006 email correspondence).

Like the WRI/WBCSD Protocol, ISO 14064 is an international standard used to prescribe GHG accounting principles. However, the ISO 14064 also certifies institutions who abide by these principles. For example, the Australian Greenhouse Challenge Plus voluntary reduction programme utilizes ISO standards as a foundation (Zwick, 2006).

The Climate Neutral Network

Numerous US based companies working to offset their emissions have linked with the Climate Neutral Network, a non profit with the goal of 'helping companies, communities and consumers achieve a net zero impact on the Earth's climate.' (www.climateneutral.com/). The organization certifies products, events, or organizations with its *Climate Cool* logo as a brand trademark. Climate Neutral Network certifies projects and also works directly with institutions to become 'net zero' emitters or to create products for the consumer market (Hall, 2004). According to the organization's website, 'A principal goal of the Network is to completely offset the greenhouse gases generated at each stage of the life-cycle of a product or service: the sourcing of its materials; its manufacturing or production; and its distribution, use, and ultimate end-of-life disposition. Companies or institutions that offset all of the gases resulting from the full spectrum of their internal operations can also receive Climate Cool enterprise certification.' (www.climateneutral.com/).

After working through Climate Neutral Network standards, the 'Climate Cool' logo is licensed to Climate Cool certified companies to utilize for their own company or product branding. Examples of events and products certified include: The rock band, Dave Matthews Band certified a recent band tour as Climate Cool; Shaklee US, a product company, offset emissions for their entire business operations, earning the title of the 'first Climate Neutral Enterprise'; and Interface carpet has created the option of buying Climate Cool carpet. Two organizations selling retail offsets, Bonneville Environmental

Foundation, and Triple E Better World Travel also cite Climate Neutral Network as a certifier (www.climateneutral.com/).

The Voluntary Carbon Standard (VCS)

In early 2006, The Climate Group, the International Trading Association (IETA), and the World Economic Forum (WEF) joined forces in creating the Voluntary Carbon Standard (VCS), which will apply to certify offset projects and credits and aims 'to provide a credible but simple set of criteria that will provide integrity to the voluntary carbon market and underpin the credible actions that already exist.'

Mark Kenber, policy director at the Climate Group, describes the standard as designed to create a basic 'quality threshold' in the market rather than compete with other standards (e.g. WBCSD/WRI GHG Protocol for Project Accounting, Gold Standard, etc.). Specifically, the Voluntary Carbon Standard looks to ensure that offset credits represent 'real, measurable, permanent, additional and independently verified' project-based emission reductions and so provide a benchmark for the rapidly growing but heterogeneous voluntary carbon market. The authors hope that, by creating a single global standard, there will be greater confidence in the voluntary market for the many players who are looking to enter and hence increase its role in driving action to reduce GHG emissions.

Project-based emission reductions meeting the VCS will become 'Voluntary Carbon Units.' (VCUs), a standardized trading unit for the voluntary carbon market and registered in an accredited voluntary carbon registry to avoid double counting. As of July, 2006, the three groups were working issues such as:

- Criteria for accrediting VCU certifiers that are not CDM Designated Operational Entities and the voluntary carbon registry;
- Criteria for the inclusion of biological and geological sinks;
- The additionality tests;
- Making project-based and performance standard-based approaches compatible;
- Governance issues, including funding the maintenance and operation of the VCS.

The process of incorporating the more than 60 written and numerous verbal comments received during the public consultation is still ongoing. Hence, elements currently described in the standard may be changed by the 2nd consultation draft, proposed for release in October 2006. Once any new changes have been approved by the VCS Steering Committee a final version will be launched, in late 2006 or early 2007.

The Gold Standard

While the VCS aims to set a basic quality threshold, the Gold Standard seeks to define the high-end market of carbon credits in both the regulatory and voluntary markets. The standard was an initiative of the World Wildlife Fund (WWF) and developed with variety of other NGOs, businesses and governmental organizations in response to the concern that the many CDM projects do not have significant sustainable development aspects. While the CDM board has screened all projects explicitly to ensure they do have sustainable development benefits, according the Michael Schlup, Director of the Gold Standard, described only 34 per cent of the CDM credits as contributing to sustainable development and the transition to sustainable energy technologies.

While the standard was originally designed to supplement CDM certification, there is now also a Gold Standard for voluntary offsets. The Gold Standard website describes several factors which make the voluntary standard unique: simplified guidelines, 'broader eligibility of host countries, lower requirements on the use of official development assistance, broader scope of eligible baseline methodologies, and no need for formal host country approval.' (www.cdmgoldstandard.org/).

All credits certified by the Gold Standard have passed through three screens:

- '*Project Type screen* – supporting non-fossil energy sources in order to contribute to the long-term change of the energy sector.
- *Additionality screen* – providing assistance in evaluating whether or not a project leads to a real net reduction of global emissions beyond a business-as-usual scenario.
- *Sustainable Development Screen* – giving guidelines and frameworks for a transparent sustainable development impact assessment, meaningful stakeholder consultations involving local communities and NGOs and potential Environmental Impact Assessments.'

After passing through these screens, CDM credit serial numbers are linked into the Gold Standard database. The standard is in the midst of creating registry procedures for VERs to ensure the quality of the credits and that they cannot be sold multiple times.

Along with providing incentives for sustainability, the Gold Standard also aims to reduce buyer's risk. According to a BASE and Gold Standard Press Release, 'Gold Standard credits mean less risk for investors and fair carbon prices for project developers whilst directly supporting sustainable development strategies in host countries.' (www.cdmgoldstandard.org). Matt Spannagle, a member of the standard's Technical Advisory committee, noted that some organizations do have a higher willingness to pay to avoid the risk of purchasing low quality credits. A number of major voluntary Gold Standard certified purchases are validating this point. For example, the FIFA World Cup initiated a 'Green Goal', which includes offsetting an estimated 100,000 tons of greenhouse gases predicted to be emitted due to event activities, mainly due to vehicle traffic. About one third of these credits bought are CDM Gold Standard carbon credits (Muenzing, 2004). Likewise HSBC bank utilized the Gold Standard when purchasing offsets to become 'the world's first carbon neutral bank.' (www.cdmgoldstandard.org).

Climate, Community & Biodiversity (CCB) Standards

One distinct feature of the Gold Standard is that it does not apply to carbon forestry projects. In contrast, the Climate, Community & Biodiversity (CCB) Standards focus exclusively on land-based carbon mitigation projects. The development of the CCB Standards was spearheaded by the Climate, Community & Biodiversity Alliance (CCBA) – a partnership between research institutions, corporations and NGOs, including, Conservation International, The Nature Conservancy, Wildlife Conservation Society, Hamburg Institute of International Economics (HWWA), British Petroleum, Weyerhaeuser, SC Johnson, Intel, CATIE, CIFOR and ICRAF – with the goal of promoting, 'integrated solutions to land management around the world.' (www.climate-standards.org).

The CCB Standards, released in May 2005, were the result of an intensive two-year international stakeholder development process, including: outside input from academia, business, environmental organizations, and development groups; field testing on four continents; and an independent peer review.

Like the Gold Standard, CCB Standards can be utilized in the voluntary or regulatory market and were created to go beyond the current CDM requirements. Specifically, the CCB Standards focus on ensuring that there is a net community and biodiversity benefit to a planned land use project.

To become certified under these standards, independent third-party auditors must determine that the project satisfies all 15 required criteria, which demonstrate the project will help mitigate climate change, conserve biodiversity, and improve socio-economic conditions for local communities. The mandatory criteria also ensure, among other things, that environmental and social monitoring programmes are in place, no invasive species are used, local stakeholders are appropriately involved in the design of the project, and there are no unresolved land tenure issues. Exceptional projects can earn Silver or Gold CCB Status depending on how many optional criteria are met. Optional criteria cover issues such as native species use, climate change adaptation, water and soil resource enhancement, and capacity building.

Project developers can use the CCB Standards for designing and certifying multiple-benefit forestry projects. In addition, investors can use the Standards as a screening tool to identify high-quality initiatives that deliver strong climate, community and biodiversity benefits while keeping risks contained. According to Toby Janson-Smith, Director of the Climate, Community & Biodiversity Alliance, projects that meet the CCB Standards can mitigate project risk in three main ways. First, CCB projects include considerations towards meeting the various resource needs of local communities (e.g., by generating sustainable livelihoods and incorporating agroforestry systems to meet local wood and agricultural needs). This integrated project approach minimizes leakage, since local people will not be driven to undertake resource-depleting activities off site. Second, CCB projects promote the creation of biodiverse landscapes and ecosystems, which can reduce the risk of natural loss (such as from pest outbreaks and fire) compared to monoculture systems. Finally, CCB certification of projects can reduce investment risk, by demonstrating the project's multiple-benefits to outside stakeholders and reducing the chance that NGOs or other disgruntled parties (including host countries) could work to discredit the investor/buyer, or deny CDM approval of the project.

Janson-Smith reports that, as of the June 2006, several dozen forestry projects around the world are using the CCB Standards, with the first projects expected to become third-party certified during the summer of 2006.

Green-e program

The Green-e Program is a widely accepted certifier of RECs in the United States. After eight years in operation, the organization has managed to secure a wide REC market segment and high levels of confidence. Green-e is currently creating a third party verification standard for RECs as carbon offsets and a certification standard and programme for retail GHG offset sellers selling both RECs and credits from other offset projects.

Green-e describes the goal of the retail GHG offset certification programme to be a similar to the Green-e certification programme for RECs, and 'to make sure things match up at the back end and to protect buyers from issues such as double counting.' The organization will not certify offset projects or offset credits, but rather will certify retail sellers. The goals of this programme will include setting minimum standards for retail offset products, insuring that customers receive quality offsets and adequate information and disclosure about their purchases, and assuring that there is no double counting.

Green-e's steps toward certification of RECs for carbon credits are driven by the fact that numerous retailers are offering Green-e certified RECs as carbon credits, but that these RECs were not certified with the purpose of being carbon offsets. The organization entered carbon credit certification through a pilot project with the retailer Terrapass. Because of Green-e's wide acceptance in the REC market, Tom Arnold, a co-founder of Terrapass, asked Green-e to conduct a third party verification for Terrapass, whose offsets include a combination of CCX and Green-e certified REC credits (Arnold, 2005). This third party verification process includes addressing and confirming the following issues:

- Balance of supply and sales: Terrapass REC and carbon purchases are in balance with our consumer and business sales obligations.
- Carbon content on RECs.
- All purchased RECs meet Green-e criteria.
- Purchases are adequately contracted, documented and have matching attestations.' (www.terrapass.com/).

The retail GHG offset certification programme is still in the midst of development. Green-e is working with a 15 member advisory group to develop a draft standard, which will be distributed from stakeholder comments late

2006 with the goal of launching the Green-e Retail GHG reduction certification program in early 2007.

References

Arnold, T. Interviewed by Katherine Hamilton December 2005

Boehmer, K. Secretary, ISO TC207 Working Group 5, Climate Change Canadian Standards Association 5060, email correspondence 7 May 2006

Hall, S. Interviewed by Katherine Hamilton May 2004

Kenber, M. (2006) 'The Voluntary Carbon Standard', Speech at *The Green-T Forum: Raising the Bar for Voluntary Environmental Credit Markets,* New York City

Kook Weng, C. and Boehmer, K. (2006) 'Launching of ISO 14064 for Greenhouse Gas Accounting and Verification', *ISO Insider*, March–April 2006

Muenzing, T. (2004) 'Scoring the Green Goal', www.greenbiz.com/news/

Schlup, M. (2005) 'Linking the CDM to Development and Poverty Reduction', *International Conference: Climate or Development,* Hamburg, Germany

Zwick, S. (2006) 'Comparing Apples and Oranges: In Search for a Standard for the Voluntary Carbon Market', *The Ecosystem Marketplace,* www.ecosystemmarketplace.com/

Websites

The CCBS website: www.climate-standards.org/

The Climate Neutral Network website: www.climateneutral.com/

The Gold Standard website: www.cdmgoldstandard.org/

The Greenhouse Gas Protocol website: www.ghgprotocol.org/

Terrapass website: www.terrapass.com/

Appendix 4

Examples of Offset Credit Retailers

Table A4.1

Name	***Project type***	***Location***	***Price in US/tCO_2e***	***Primary markets***
American Forests	Forestry	US	$3.00	Individuals/institutions
AtmosClear Climate Club	Landfill/methane	US	$3.50 to $25.00 (w/membership)	Individuals
AtmosFair	Fossil fuel emissions reductions	Germany	$19.50	Individuals
Australian Carbon Biosequestration Initiative	Local forestry	Australia	Varies by partnership	Australian institutions
Bonneville Environmental Foundation	RECs	US	$14.50 to $29.00	Individuals/institutions
Business for Climate	Forestry	Netherlands	$12.50 to $17.00	Individuals/institutions
Carbon Clear	Mix	UK	$14.00 to $30.00	Individuals
Carbonfund	Mix	US	$5.50	Individuals/institutions
The Carbon Neutral Company	Mix	UK	$12.00 to $22.00	Individuals/institutions
Certified Clean Car/ PVUSAsolar	RECs	US	$6.00	Individuals
Cleanairpass	RECs and mix	Canada	$4.50 to $9.00	Individuals
Cleaner and Greener	Mix	USA	Varies	Individuals/institutions
Climate Care	Mix	UK	$12.50	Individuals/institutions
Climate Change Consulting	Livestock/methane	Germany	$12.50 to $13.00	Institutions
Climate Friendly	RECs	Australia	$16.00 to $19.00	Individuals/institutions
Climate Save	RECs	US	N/A	Individuals/institutions
The Climate Trust/ Mercy Trust	Fossil fuel emissions reductions	US	$6.00 to $10.00	Individuals/ institutions/Oregon Regulatory

Table A4.1 *Continued*

Name	*Project type*	*Location*	*Price in US/tCO_2e*	*Primary markets*
CO_2 Australia	Forestry (eucalypt)	Australia	N/A	Institutions/ compliance
CO_2 Balance	Forestry	UK	N/A	Individuals/institutions
CO_2OL Planet	Native forestry	Germany	$12.50 to $15.50	Individuals/institutions
CO_2OL-USA	Native forestry	US	$10.00	Individuals/institutions
Conservation International	Forestry	US	$5.00 to $20.00	Institutions
The Conservation Fund: Go Zero	Native forestry	US	$4.00	Individuals/institutions
Drive Green/Ag- Cert	Livestock/ methane	US	$5.00 to $7.00	Individuals/compliance
Drive Neutral	CCX	US	$7.50 and up	Individuals
EBEX21	Native forestry	New Zealand	$9.00 to $9.50	Institutions
E-BlueHorizons	Methane/forestry	US	$5.00	Individuals/institutions
Environmental Synergy	Native Forestry	US	$2.00	Institutions
Envirotrade/Plan Vivo/ ECCM/	Forestry	Scotland	$6.50 to $19.00	Individuals/institutions
Green Fleet	Native Forestry	Australia	$7.00 to $7.50	Individuals/institutions
Grow A Forest	Forestry	England	N/A	Institutions
MyClimate	Mix	Switzerland	$30.00	Individuals
Native Energy	RECs	USA	$13.50	Individuals
Natsource	HFC-23, Enhanced Oil Recovery, Fuel switch	USA	$4.00	Individuals, broker
Offsetters	CCX	Canada	$14.50	Individuals
Primaklima	Forestry	Germany	$2.00	Individuals
Solar Electric Light Fund (SELF)	Off-grid Solar Energy	USA	$10	Institutions
Sustainable Travel International	RECs through myclimate	US	$17.50	Individuals
TerraPass	RECs/CCX	US	$8.00 to $11.00	Individuals/institutions
TIST	Forestry and agriculture	US	$20.00	Individuals
Trees for the Future	Forestry	US	$0.10	Individuals

Note: Listed prices are approximate and are based upon research conducted in late 2005, early 2006. Most but not all prices were checked in mid-2006, when currency conversions were made using www.xe.com/ucc/convert.cgi and prices were rounded to the nearest half dollar. Prices checked against www.ecobusinesslinks.com/carbon_offset_wind_credits_carbon_reduction.htm in August 2006.

American Forests

www.americanforests.org

Location: Washington, D.C.

Business Model: American Forests is the nation's oldest nonprofit citizens' conservation organization. Since 1990, American Forests' Global ReLeaf campaign has been planting native trees in rural and urban ecosystem restoration projects across the United States and around the world. The campaign plants trees where they are desperately needed such as along hillsides to reduce erosion and streams to prevent polluted runoff and sedimentation as well as other ecologically significant areas. About 85 per cent of American Forests' tree-planting projects occur in the United States and 15 per cent are international efforts. All are conducted in cooperation with local partners, foresters, or natural resource experts. American Forests offers customers the opportunity to use an online carbon calculator in order to calculate the emissions associated with their daily lifestyle and then offset them by paying to plant trees (through the Global ReLeaf campaign) that will sequester the equivalent amount of carbon dioxide.

Pricing: US$1.00 per tree; $3.00 per tCO_2e

Volume: N/A

Primary Markets: Individuals and businesses

* * * * *

AtmosClear Climate Club

www.atmosclear.org

Location: Northborough, Massachusetts, USA

Business Model: AtmosClear Climate Club is a for-profit company that provides offsets for individuals and institutions. Consumers can become an Atmosclear Climate Club member and/or purchase credits sold in blocks of 1, 3, 6, 12 or 25 tons. Customers can calculate their emissions online. Each membership comes with a certificate with serial numbers for offsets purchased, a member benefits card, an UndoYourCO_2 sticker, annual membership sticker and AtmosClear Climate Club magnet. Members have access to some special deals from sponsors, such as ski resorts and can purchase offsets for friends and family. AtmosClear's carbon offsets (described as Emission Reduction Credits by the company) are from a methane trapping and renewable energy project at the Des Plaines Landfill based Northwest of Chicago, Illinois and have third party verification by Environmental Resources Trust.

Pricing: US$3.50–$25.00 (w/membership) per tCO_2e

Partners and Clients: The organization has partnerships with organizations such as Arapahoe Basin Ski Area, Bear Valley Mountain Resort, Clear Channel Communications and Better World Club. It was selected by Environmental Defense as an approved offset credit seller.

Volume: N/A

Primary Markets: Individual consumers

* * * * *

Atmosfair

www.atmosfair.de/index.php?id=0&L=3

Location: Bonn and Berlin, Germany

Business Model: Atmosfair provides offsets for GHG created by air travel. Passengers can buy an Atmosfair certificate at certified travel agents (those that are part of the German Forum Anders Reisen, a tourism trade association) or through the internet. Passengers determine a flight's GHG emissions through Atmosfair's online calculator and then purchase offset certificates. (Those paying tax in Germany can also receive tax reduction receipts). Atmosfair then invests money raised in Gold Standard CDM certified climate protection projects. Projects currently include electricity from waste at the University of Rio (Brazil), solar heaters for kitchens at schools, hospitals and temples in India and electricity and heating for a residential area in South Africa. Under the CDM mechanism, the projects are carried out according to Kyoto rules and are monitored by UN accredited technical organizations.

Partners and Clients: Atmosfair claims to be the first organization in the world to offer a Gold Standard project certified in accordance with the UN procedure.

Pricing: €15.00 per tCO_2e

Volume: 6000tCO_2 per year

Primary Markets: Leisure and business travelers, businesses/organizations

* * * * *

Australian Carbon Biosequestration Initiative (Big Green Umbrella)

www.biggreenumbrella.org.au/index.php

Location: Adelaide, Australia

Business Model: The Australian Carbon Biosequestration Initiative is a non-profit organization that links businesses who want to offset GHG emissions with environmental and community groups involved with revegetation. Under the Big Green Umbrella Project, the organization aims to plant 200,000 hectares of native vegetation in Australia funded by offsetting 60 million tCO_2. Rather than charging per ton of CO_2 offset, Big Green Umbrella charges the emitter per product and binds the emitter to the landowner providing the sequestration service. Kyoto rules are followed.

Partners and Clients: SAFF, a biofuel retailer serving 50 outlets, is working with the Big Green Umbrella to offset emissions from its Green Fuel product. Greening Australia has designed and will implement SAFF's tree planting programme, which is guaranteed for five years.

Pricing: Unique to each project

Volume: 1000tCO_2e in 2005

Primary Markets: Australian businesses, local government authorities

* * * * *

Bonneville Environmental Foundation

www.b-e-f.org/index.shtm

Location: Portland, Oregon, USA

Business Model: Bonneville Environmental Foundation (BEF) is a non-profit organization that markets green power products to public utilities, businesses, government agencies and individuals. BEF provides project finance and design for renewable, distributed energy generation technologies in the US through individual and business who wish to offset carbon emissions. Products include renewable energy credits called Green Tags (RECs) from wind, solar and biomass energy with 1 Green Tag equaling 1MWh of renewable energy entering the grid. Revenue pays for metered output from renewable energy sources and is reinvested in BEF-supported projects. The foundation also funds watershed restoration programmes through tree planting and water monitoring activities.

Partners and Clients: BEF's Green Tags are certified by Green-e (www.green-e.org), the main US body for renewable energy verification and certification. About half of BEF's clients are utilities, half are businesses and less than 5 per cent are individuals. Clients include Portland General Electric, Oregon State University and Climate Solutions. BEF has also partnered with a variety of ski areas to sell Green Tags and promote the 'Keep Winter Cool' campaign.

Pricing: US$14.50 to $29.00 per tCO_2e

Volume: 175,000tCO_2e in 2005 (700,000tCO_2e since 1998)

Primary Markets: US-based public utilities, schools/universities, non-profit organizations, businesses, government organizations

Business for Climate

www.bfclimate.nl/Eng/index_E.html

Location: The Netherlands

Business Model: Business for Climate allows businesses to become climate neutral or to brand climate neutral products by buying carbon credits from sustainable forestry projects managed by a partner organization, the Face Foundation (www.stichtingface.nl/index.php?lang=uk). The foundation has restored approximately 50,000 hectares since 1998 in collaboration with national parks in the Czech Republic and Uganda, a large concession in Malaysia and landowners in the Netherlands and Ecuador.

Partners and Clients: Projects are selected for additionality, social acceptability and cost effectiveness and are submitted for third-party verification by Societe General de Surveillance to the Forest Stewardship Council's Greenhouse Gas Verification and Certification scheme, which registers sequestration in the Schedule of Projected Emission Reduction Units. While not recognized as CDM projects, Face uses the same criteria for identification and implementation. Customers include the City of Rotterdam and Dutch power companies.

Pricing: €13.00 per tCO_2e (individuals) and €10.00 per tCO_2e (businesses)

Volume: N/A

Primary Markets: Small businesses, government, power companies, individuals

* * * * *

Carbon Clear

Business Model: Carbon Clear is a for-profit company that sells a variety of carbon offset packages for drivers and frequent flyers. Carbon Clear also offers a variety of gift ideas (including, among other things, carbon offsets for diapers) and allows clients to design custom offset packages. As a buyer, Carbon Clear supports a basket (or portfolio) of activities around the world that reduce global pollution. According to the website, Carbon Clear follows, 'A simple philosophy in our choice of projects: we invest in projects that provide strong social and environmental benefits to communities in developing countries, as well as global climate benefits.' In particular, Carbon Clear looks for projects with low bureaucratic overhead and long-term benefits to communities and biodiversity.

Partners and Clients: Carbon Clear works with TIST and several other project developers working in the developing world.

Pricing: For businesses, prices range from £7.50–9.50. For retail sales to individuals, prices range from £10–15. All prices are volume dependent.

Volume: Carbon Clear did not begin trading until mid-December 2005, so no volumes are available yet.

Primary Markets: Businesses and individuals

* * * * *

Carbonfund.org

www.carbonfund.org

Location: Silver Spring, Maryland, USA

Business Model: Carbonfund.org is a non-profit organization composed of environmental professionals that follows the guideline of 'Reduce What You Can, Offset What You Can't'™. Carbonfund.org helps individuals and companies assess their carbon footprint, reduce their emissions, and offset the rest. Carbonfund.org sources carbon credits from energy efficiency, renewable energy and sequestration projects and retires them. Individuals and businesses contribute to Carbonfund.org to offset their carbon footprint, which is determined by Carbonfund.org's online calculator or via assistance from their staff. Carbonfund maintains contact with project developers throughout the world and selects offset projects based on a variety of criteria, including price, quality, certification and other social benefits. It also purchases credits through wholesalers. Carbonfund.org follows a 'Your Carbon, Your Choice' model by allowing contributors to choose what type of offsets they would like to support.

Carbonfund's business has increased many times over since 2004, when it offset a few thousand tonnes of CO_2. The organization attributes this to its low cost, simplicity and non-profit status.

Partners and Clients: Environmental Resources Trust (ERT) audits Carbonfund.org's baseline assessment practices, and energy and project verification is provided by Green-e, ERT, and CCX. Carbonfund.org's entire portfolio of offsets is audited by ERT. Carbonfund is a member of the EPA's Green Power Network, the Chicago Climate Exchange, and Ceres.

Pricing: US$5.50 per tCO_2e

Volume: 100,000 plus tCO_2e

Primary Markets: Businesses, non-profits and individuals

* * * * *

The CarbonNeutral Company

www.carbonneutral.com

Location: London, England

Business Model: The CarbonNeutral Company (formerly Future Forests) is primarily a consultancy and brokerage house offering a range of carbon expertise and products, from carbon management for corporate and government clients to climate-related gifts direct to consumers. It operates under the branded Carbon-Neutral Protocol, a third-party verified standard that codifies the company's methodology for emission reductions. The focus to date has been on projects outside the Kyoto mechanisms, thus offering VERs to clients, but the company is expanding into CDM projects in order to provide CERs as well.

To provide offsets, CarbonNeutral sources and invests in renewable energy, energy efficiency and forestry projects in Europe, North and Central America, the Indian sub-continent and Africa. They are managed by third party partners and verified against the CarbonNeutral Protocol by KPMG. Reforestation and afforestation are considered acceptable offsets provided they are commercially or legally additional, were established after 1 January 2000 and deliver emissions reductions over a non-project baseline. Projects must also provide a social, environmental or economic benefit, for example contributing to biodiversity. In 2004, 50 per cent of CarbonNeutral's reduction projects were technological and 50 per cent were sinks, but this is expected to shift toward 80 per cent technological and 20 per cent sinks in 2005. The company has planted more than 2.5 million trees across the world, establishing 80 forests in the UK in addition to Mexico, India, Germany, North America and Canada.

Partners and Clients: CarbonNeutral sold 1,637tCO_2e to Volvo in 2002. It has also traded with Avis Europe, Swiss Re, Barclays Bank, O2 and MTV. Additionally, CarbonNeutral has signed up over 14,000 individuals to offset car rental and flight emissions and emissions associated with manufacturing CDs for musicians.

Pricing: US$12.00–22.00 per t$CO_2$e (bulk institutional prices), $16.00–20.00t$CO_2$e (retail prices)

Volume: 120,000tCO_2e in 2004 (750,000tCO_2e to date)

Primary Markets: Business, consumers

* * * * *

Certified Clean Car

www.certifiedcleancar.com

Location: San Francisco, California, USA

Business Model: The Certified Clean Car programme enables drivers to offset carbon emissions by purchasing renewable energy credits (RECs) and carbon credits. Fifty percent of the credits are provided through the Green-e Renewable Energy Certification Program administered by the US-based Center for Resource Solutions, and 50 per cent are provided through purchases on the

CCX. Certified Clean Car is run by Renewable Ventures LLC, a renewa energy investment and management company which finances and operate renewable energy power plants.

Pricing: $6.00 per tCO_2e

Volume: 190tCO_2e in 2005

Primary Markets: Businesses and individuals

* * * * *

Climate Wedge Limited Oy

http://www.climatewedge.com/

Location: London

Business Model: Climate Wedge Ltd Oy is a scientific adviser to the Cheyne Carbon Fund. Cheyne Capital Management Ltd launched the Cheyne Carbon Fund in August 2005. Cheyne Capital Management Ltd manages the Carbon Fund. The Carbon Fund has a globally diversified portfolio of emissions reductions for use as carbon offsets by corporate and institutional buyers wishing to offer carbon offset products and services to their customers, or to offset their direct emissions. Climate Wedge aims to drive and support novel ways in which robust offsets can be used and recognized as a meaningful response option to mitigating corporate GHG emissions across all sectors and regions.

Primary Markets: Business and other organizations

* * * * *

Cleaner and Greener

www.cleanerandgreener.org

Location: Madison, Wisconsin, USA

Business Model: Cleaner and Greener is a non-profit organization of the Leonardo Academy that acts as a broker between helps individuals, businesses, organizations, schools and universities who want to reduce emissions and renewable energy providers. Through the organization's event certification programme, event organizers calculate emissions generated by travel and electricity usage and determine appropriate offset actions. The Leonardo Academy also helps companies donate and permanently retire emission reductions certificates and allowances to the Cleaner and Greener Program and is developing a programme to offer emission reductions certificates to businesses and individuals who undertake energy efficiency, renewable energy and other emission reduction actions.

Pricing: N/A

lume: N/A

rimary Markets: Individuals and small/medium-sized businesses

* * * * *

Climate Save

www.climatesave.com

Location: Westborough, Massachusetts, US

Business Model: Climate Save partners with Green-e to provide Green-e certified RECs to consumers. The company currently supports wind, solar and hydro projects in Kansas, New York and New England.

Projects, Partners and Clients: Green-e

Pricing: US$8.75 for 500 kWh of RECS

Volume: N/A

Primary Markets: Individuals

* * * * *

Clean Air Pass

www.cleanairpass.com

Location: Toronto, Canada

Business Model: Clean Air Pass is a for-profit organization focused on providing credits for individuals to offset their vehicle use. After calculating their emissions online, buyers receive a sticker for their vehicles. Credits are currently purchased from CCX, and may include RECs in the future.

Pricing: $5.00–$10.00 (CAD) per tCO_2e

Volume: 2100tCO_2e

Primary Markets: Individuals offsetting vehicles

* * * * *

Climate Care

www.climatecare.org

Location: Oxford, England

Business Model: Climate Care is a for-profit company selling carbon offsets to individuals and businesses and using the 'CO_2 liability' to fund and manage offset projects. Projects include energy efficiency, renewable energy and forestry (20 per cent) and are verified by third parties, generating VERs not in accordance with Kyoto or EU ETS rules. This deliberate strategy is to create funding for projects that cannot be used to meet national EU targets and would not have otherwise occurred. For businesses, Climate Care helps determine offset goals and current emissions and purchases credits on behalf of clients' products, operations and events. Individuals can use an online calculator to offset air travel, home and car emissions.

Climate Care is particularly dedicated to transparency, publishing a detailed annual financial report on its web site. The 2004 report indicates that 40–45 per cent of revenues were spent directly on projects, and sales have doubled each year since 2002. Climate Care's projects are primarily in non-Annex B countries and include efforts such as distributing efficient cooking stoves in Honduras and Bangladesh, restoring a rainforest in Uganda and installing efficient lighting in South African households.

Partners and Clients: A wide range of English and global clients includes the Association of British Travel Agents, The Guardian newspaper, Shell-Russia, Interface Carpets and the Liberal Democrats. The company is looking for additional projects to fund.

Pricing: £6.60 per tCO_2e

Volume: 97,000tCO_2e

Primary Markets: Businesses, individuals, project managers

* * * * *

Climate Change Consulting (3C)

www.3c-company.com/index_en.htm

Location: Frankfurt, Germany

Business Model: Climate Change Consulting (3C) offers a full range of services to businesses in the compliance and voluntary carbon markets, including a voluntary programme to offset travel, operations, products and event emissions. Through the Carbon Neutral programme, 3C develops customized climate neutral strategies for businesses and organizes carbon offsets, which are then retired. These offsets are generated by the Emission Reduction Project Biogas Plant Gundorf in Germany, which displaces open-air storage by technical treatment of cattle manure in bio-methanisation plants. The additionality and other quality standards of the plant's ERCs are verified by a third party and do not conform to Kyoto rules.

Partners and Clients: 3C is responsible for the climate neutralization of the 2006 World Cup for which it needs Gold Standard CDM certificates. It is also actively looking for other projects, as client demand for ERCs is high and growing. Other clients and partners include major German and international companies, such as T-Mobile, Lufthansa, Allianz, HSBC and 20th Century Fox.

Pricing: €10.00 per tCO_2e

Volume: 300,000tCO_2e in 2005
Primary Market(s): business and corporations

* * * * *

Climate Friendly

www.climatefriendly.com

Location: Sydney and Byron Bay, New South Wales, Australia

Business Model: Climate Friendly provides a platform for businesses and individuals to offset their household, electricity, travel and product/operations carbon emissions through the purchase of renewable energy carbon offsets. The company's focus is on creating demand for a climate neutral energy supply. While individuals and businesses seem increasingly interested in becoming carbon neutral, sales remain low due to long lead times for commercial sales (from figuring a carbon footprint to budgeting for offsets and then purchasing) and limited demand for voluntary offsets. Carbon credits are generated by Australian government approved Green Power wind energy and the Te Apiti Wind Farm in New Zealand, which is a CDM Gold Standard operation, as well as from projects under the NSW GGAS. Climate Friendly is looking for additional verified emission saving projects, particularly renewable energy and energy efficiency.

Partners and Clients: Clients include Slingfings Bags, the Ethical Investment Association, the World Wide Fund for Nature Australia and Szencorp's Melbourne office building.

Pricing: US$16.00–$19.00

Volume: 2300tCO_2e

Primary Markets: Businesses and individuals

* * * * *

The Climate Trust

www.climatetrust.org

Location: Portland, Oregon, USA

Business Model: The Climate Trust is a non-profit organization investing in emissions reduction projects on behalf of businesses, individuals, regulators and power plants and is considered one of the largest offset buyers in the US market. It acts in somewhat of a wholesaler capacity in that it receives from emitters, then oversees the request for proposal and screening pr for projects, awards funding, manages projects over their lifetime and retr credits on behalf of emitters. Generated credits are exclusively owned b The Climate Trust.

The organization was started in order to service Oregon power and utility companies. New power stations in Oregon are required by law to meet emissions standards and can do so by purchasing offsets. In addition to this Oregon Carbon Dioxide Offset Program, the Trust now also runs a GHG Offset Partnership Program in which large emitters can acquire offsets as a corporate asset for use in present or future mitigation measures and businesses can offset emissions through a tax deductible donation. Individuals can work with the Trust through carboncounter.org to calculate emissions and purchase offsets.

The Climate Trust's project portfolio includes 12 energy efficiency, renewable energy, sequestration, cogeneration, material substitution and transportation efficiency projects, including energy efficiency upgrades at an Oregon paper company, wind farms in Oregon and Washington, Ecuadorian rainforest restoration and cogeneration of heat energy and electrical power at a lumber mill. The Climate Trust periodically solicits requests for proposals for new offset projects and is currently undergoing a process to allocate $30 million of funding.

Partners and Clients: The Climate Trust works with Oregon Power Plant Offset Program, the Large Emitter Offset Acquisition Program, and a variety of foundations. Over 30 organizations, such as Delta Airlines, Patagonia, and Nike, have joined the Climate Trust's Donate to Offset programme.

Pricing: US$6.00–$10.00 per tCO_2e

Volume: This programme has offset 4.3 million tCO_2e to date

Primary Markets: Utility and manufacturing companies, power plants, businesses and individuals

* * * * *

Conservation International

www.conservation.org

Location: Headquartered in Washington, D.C., US

Business Model: Conservation International is an international non- profit conservation organization. By incorporating the science of climate change into conservation strategies, Conservation International (CI) is working to demonstrate that CO_2 emissions can be reduced not only by restoring natural forests that absorb CO_2, but also by preventing the release of greenhouse gases when land and forests are cleared or burned (estimated to be 20 per cent of annual global emissions) particularly in Biodiversity Hotspots.

…hrough its Center for Environmental Leadership in Business (CELB), CI …ages industry in this effort and offers cost-effective options for businesses to …set their emissions. CI maintains a portfolio of land-based Conservation …arbon offset projects, and over 70 per cent of offset funding goes directly to these projects. The center has developed a portfolio of carbon offset projects in Ecuador, Madagascar, China, Indonesia and the Philippines. CELB works with large organizations and individuals to offset their emissions. For example, CELB recently partnered with Pearl Jam to offset the band's 2006 World Tour. Individuals can calculate their carbon footprint on CI's website and donate $10 per tCO_2e to offset their emissions.

In addition, CELB with many partner companies and non-profits has created the Climate, Community & Biodiversity Standards (CCB Standards) to develop, test and promote high quality land-use, land-use change and forestry (LULUCF) carbon offsets.

Projects, Partners and Clients: Partner organizations include the Government of Madagascar, China's State Forestry Administration, Wildlife Conservation Society, Maquipucuna Foundation, Jatun Sacha Foundation and local community groups manage these projects locally. The World Bank, The Climate Trust, S.C. Johnson, Imperial Tobacco, NAVTEQ, Pearl Jam and Mitsubishi have been major funding partners.

Pricing: US$5.00–$20.00 per tCO_2e

Volume: Variable with many returning annual clients purchasing tens of thousands of tCO_2e per year

Primary Markets: Large and medium-sized businesses, financial institutions, governments, and individual donors

* * * * *

The Conservation Fund

www.conservationfund.org/

Location: Arlington, Virginia, USA

Business Model: The Conservation Fund is a non-membership, non-advocacy conservation organization working on issues such as land conservation, sustainable business and industry, and leadership training. Through its Carbon Sequestration programme the organization works with companies and public agencies to acquire and reforest marginal agricultural lands across the Southeast, to offsetting carbon emissions and restoring wildlife habitat. Thus far the Fund and its partners have purchased more than 26,000 acres and planted more than five million trees. At the retail level the organization receives donations for carbon credits from its Go Zero programme. Where customers calculate their emissions online and then donate to the Fund to pay for native tree planting.

Partners and Clients: The fund works with numerous organizations on its sequestration programmes, such as American Electric Power Company, Inc., ChevronTexaco Corporation, Cinergy Corporation, DTE Energy, Entergy, Environmental Synergy, Inc., PowerTree Carbon Company LLC, Reliant Energy, Winrock International

Pricing: US$4.00 per tCO_2e

Volume: N/A

Primary Markets: Large companies, individuals

* * * * *

CO_2 Australia

www.co2australia.com.au/profile.htm

Location: Melbourne, Victoria, Australia

Business Model: CO_2 Australia has launched the CO_2 Australia Carbon Sequestration Program to establish long-term, large-scale mallee eucalypt plantations to provision carbon credits for clients. The company aims to sell credits into the compliance and voluntary carbon markets both in Australia and internationally. Initial efforts have identified a demand for 800,000 hectares of carbon sinks, which the company will be scaling up over the next 3–4 years.

Pricing: N/A

Volume: 800,000 hectares for procurement

Primary Markets: Businesses in the compliance and voluntary markets

* * * * *

Co2balance

www.co2balance.com/home.php

Location: Somerset, England

Business Model: Co2balance works with businesses and individuals to reduce carbon impacts and offset remaining car, air and household emissions through carbon credits created by trees and land that the company owns. Activities are verified by Bournemouth University, but the criteria for verification are unclear.

Projects, Partners and Clients: Co2balance works primarily with UK-based businesses and government organizations to offset events and operations.

Pricing: N/A

Volumes: N/A

Primary Markets: Businesses and individuals

CO_2OL Planet

http://co2ol.de/index.php?id=103&L=3

Location: Bonn, Germany

Business Model: CO_2OL Planet allows businesses and individuals to neutralize carbon emissions through offsets created by native forest plantations in Panama, which are established and operated under third party certification using Forest Stewardship Council (FSC) norms. By buying CO_2OL CO_2-Certificates, participants can offset travel, household, car, event, shopping, operations and other activities. These certificates were the first reforestation certificates traded through Natsource, an international brokerage house.

Partners and Clients: CO_2OL partners with Futuro Forestal S.A., a German–Panamanian forest service company that has reforested 600 hectares of tropical forests in Panama in the last 10 years. These forests produce high-value tropical hardwoods in addition to carbon credits and non-timber forest products within a sustainable environment.

Pricing: €10.00–12.00 per tCO_2e

Volume: N/A

Primary Markets: Business and individuals

* * * * *

CO_2OL-USA

www.co2ol-usa.com/pages/176792/index.htm

Location: Missoula, Montana, USA

Business Model: CO_2OL-USA establishes native species forests on degraded and abandoned lands in Central America to provide local employment and income from forestry and a stream of verified carbon credits. Forestry activities occur for 25 years after which the forest is transferred to the members of the surrounding community under conservation easement to be managed as a communal land trust. CO_2OL-USA currently does self-certification of carbon credits but is in the process of receiving third-party certification through Swiss Société Générale de Surveillance. Once the audit is complete, CO_2OL-USA's activities will hold certifications for both forest management activities (certified by SmartWood and the Forestry Stewardship Council) and carbon accounting.

Carbon credits generated by CO_2OL-USA receive unique identification numbers, linking them to a specific plot of land and a specific year. The purchase of offsets entitles clients to the purchase of appropriate land; survey; land registration with the pertinent national authority; fencing; forest management planning; fire breaks; nursery work; planting; production organic manure; replanting in the event of initial mortality; and the care and maintenance of the establishing forest for 25 years, including fire control, phytosanitary control, and employee training and capacity building.

Pricing: US$10.00 per tCO_2e

Volume: N/A

Primary Markets: Individuals and institutions

* * * * *

Drive Green (Agcert)

www.agcert.com

www.drivinggreen.com/

Location: International, Base office: Dublin, Ireland, Drive Green: Florida, USA

Business Model: Drive Green is the retail arm of Agcert, a multinational company which generates large scale greenhouse gas (GHG) emission reductions by reducing greenhouse gas emissions on livestock farms using livestock waste management technology, such as anaerobic digestion, to capture and flare methane emissions. AgCert's proprietary systems and processes include a United Nations-approved methodology for the reduction of GHG emissions from modified animal waste management systems. The company sells credits under the CDM, as well as to the voluntary market. Drive Green was created for individuals to offset emissions from driving. Individuals can calculate their vehicles emissions online and receive a bumper sticker after purchasing credits.

Partners and Clients: This Natsource programme was selected by Environmental Defense as an approved offset seller.

Pricing: US$5.00–$7.00 per tCO_2e

Volume: 3612tCO_2e (as of July 2006)

Primary Markets: Individuals (Drive Green) CDM and wholesale voluntary (Agcert)

* * * * *

DriveNeutral

www.driveneutral.org

Location: San Francisco, California, USA

siness Model: *Drive*Neutral launched in October 2005 and allows motorists to fset their vehicular emissions by purchasing certificates, which represent carbon credits bought through the CCX and retired. The company, which is run by business students from the Presidio School of Management, purchases blocks of carbon credits, allowing individuals to access the CCX's credits reserved for larger institutions. In the future, *Drive*Neutral plans to invest in project-based transactions, but is initially focused on promoting and stimulating demand for credits via the CCX.

Partners and Clients: *Drive*Neutral is run by the Presidio School of Management, an associate member of the CCX.

Pricing: US$7.50 per tCO_2e and up

Volume: $1000tCO_2e$ by mid-2006

Primary Markets: Individuals

* * * * *

EBEX21

www.ebex21.co.nz

Location: Lincoln, New Zealand

Business Model: EBEX21 (Emissions/Biodiversity Exchange in the 21st century) provides tools and services for businesses and individuals to measure, manage and mitigate their energy use and GHG emissions. Operated by Landcare Research New Zealand, the project channels funds from participants to New Zealand landowners regenerating native forests on degraded land. These efforts are Kyoto certified under Article 3.3 LULUCF, and landowners are required to seek a covenant to protect the forest into perpetuity under schemes such as the Queen Elizabeth II National Trust. EBEX21 does not own the credits but acts as an agent between landowners and purchasers. It also provides a credit registration and auditing service to verify how many carbon credits each landowner has available to sell and their biodiversity value.

EBEX21 currently has about $30,000tCO_2$ per year of potential credits available to sell through landowners' efforts, but because of low demand, these credits have not been registered or contracted for sale.

Partners and Clients: EBEX21 clients are primarily New Zealand-based small-medium enterprises.

Pricing: NZ$15.00 per tCO_2e (80 per cent passed on to landowner)

Volume: $5000tCO_2e$

Primary Markets: New Zealand-based businesses and individuals

E-Blue Horizons LLC

www.e-bluehorizons.com/

Location: USA

Business Model: E-Blue Horizons sells credits for retirement generated by the capture and destruction of methane at municipal solid waste landfills where the active capture and use of such methane is not mandated. This process also generates renewable energy. One half of the net proceeds from purchases are then donated to The Conservation Fund, a non-profit working in the United States to promote reforestation and preserve sensitive wildlife habitats, working landscapes, recreation areas, and open space.

Partners and Clients: Donates part of profits to The Conservation Fund. It was selected by Environmental Defense as an approved offset credit seller.

Pricing: US$5.00 per tCO_2e

Volume: N/A

Primary Markets: Individuals

* * * * *

Environmental Synergy, Inc.

www.environmental-synergy.com/main.html

Location: Atlanta, Georgia, USA

Business Model: Environmental Synergy, Inc. (ESI) is a service organization providing reforestation and carbon quantification services to corporate clients to offset carbon emissions and promote sustainable forestry. The company's turnkey project development includes land acquisition (usually co-funded by federal or state conservation agencies), tree planting and carbon monitoring through year ten of the project. Clients calculate this upfront project cost over the 70-year carbon sequestration period, resulting in a lower cost per ton than net present value calculations. ESI focuses primarily on bottomland hardwood restoration in the ecologically altered region of the Lower Mississippi River Valley in the US.

Partners and Clients: In 2005 Texaco invested $900,000 in a 70-year reforestation project that will remove 800,000tCO_2e from the atmosphere.

Pricing: US$2.00 per tCO_2e (net present value figured at 4.80tCO_2e$, NPV figured at a six per cent discount rate and assuming a constant delivery of tons of carbon credits over time.

Volume: ESI has reforested 70,000 acres of bottomland hardwood forests since 1999. Each acre is expected to sequester 400tCO_2e over a 70-year period.

Primary Markets: Business

Envirotrade – Plan Vivo

www.envirotrade.co.uk/index.html

Location: London, England

Business Model: Envirotrade is a for-profit business that uses a social-forestry model to address climate change and sustainability in the developing world. Its Plan Vivo System plans, manages, monitors and verifies the supply of carbon offsets from small farmers who plant trees on their land. Envirotrade sells these verified credits (to clients directly or to other retailers), and a percentage of the revenues raised is paid back to farmers, creating monetary value for the ecosystem services of their land (in addition to a sustainable tree harvest). Local trust funds register farmers' plans for forestry developments, which are then assessed for their carbon sequestration potential and form the basis of carbon service agreements between buyers and sellers. Farmers and communities are encouraged to register and establish additional areas in a reserve carbon fund, which are drawn on to underwrite the principal transactions. Projects are not Kyoto-compliant.

Partners and Clients: The Plan Vivo System was created in Chiapas, Mexico, by the Edinburgh Centre for Carbon Management and has expanded to rehabilitate habitat in Mozambique in addition to programmes in Uganda and India.

Pricing: £3.50–10.00 per tCO_2e

Volumes: N/A

Primary Markets: Individuals

* * * * *

Greenfleet

www.greenfleet.com.au

Location: Koonwarra, Victoria, Australia

Business Model: Greenfleet plants trees to offset car emissions from individuals and corporate and government fleets. For A$40 per vehicle, per year Greenfleet plants 17 trees in native forests around Australia using ex-ante accounting in which the trees absorb approximately one year's worth of car emissions ($4.3tCO_2$) over their 50-year lifespan. Locations are chosen for their environmental attributes, with a goal of re-establishing a mix of native species from seeds collected in the local area to provide additional ecological benefits, such as reducing salinity and soil erosion and providing habitat for native species. The company is working toward measuring the carbon uptake from its efforts based on Kyoto rules but at present the work is self-verified.

Partners and Clients: Greenfleet has attracted a wide range of clients, includi[ng] federal, state and local Australian government organizations, internationa[l] corporations with operations in Australia and individuals.

Pricing: AU $9.00 per tCO_2 (net present value figured at $21.50 per tCO_2, NPV figured at a six per cent discount rate and assuming a constant delivery of carbon credits over time).

Volume: Since 1997, Greenfleet has planted more than 2.3 million trees equaling approximately 616,400tCO_2 of future offsets.

Primary Markets: Businesses and individuals

* * * * *

Grow a Forest

www.growaforest.com

Location: Lancashire, England

Business Model: Grow a Forest raises funds from individuals and businesses wishing to offset personal carbon emissions through its Carbon Reversal programme. The non-profit, volunteer-run business uses funds to purchase new land to grow wholly owned forests for public recreational and educational use and to invest in renewable/sustainable energy projects. Its emissions reductions are self-verified and forests are self-managed. Grow a Forest is aiming to plant 200 trees per month in a ten-acre plot it owns in Lancashire, England. One thousand trees were planted there in 2005.

Partners and Clients: Clients include primarily small, environmental-oriented companies wishing to offset UK-based business travel, operations and products.

Pricing: unknown

Volume: 1595tCO_2e in 2005

Primary Markets: Businesses and individuals

* * * * *

The international small group and tree planting program (TIST)

www.tist.org

Location: Tulsa, Oklahoma, USA

Business Model: TIST creates an administration and communication structure for small groups of subsistence farmers to achieve sustainable development goals through forestry and agriculture. Trees from these efforts create carbon credits, and small cash stipends are deposited into bank accounts opened by communities. Individuals can buy carbon credits in support of these efforts.

ST currently has established projects in Tanzania and India and new projects in Uganda and Kenya with over local 20,000 participants.

Pricing: US$20.00 per tCO_2e

Volume: 2000tCO_2e per year

Primary Markets: Individuals

* * * * *

MyClimate

www.myclimate.org/EN/index.php

Location: Zurich, Switzerland

Business Model: MyClimate is a branded product that allows individuals and businesses to offset primarily travel emissions. It is represented to the German market through the MyClimate foundation and to the American market through Sustainable Travel International and can be purchased through associated travel agents or online. The carbon offsets created by these efforts are verified by the Swiss Federal Institute of Technology based on criteria that are in accordance with the CDM Gold Standard project design document. However, the projects are not certified CDM due to their small scale and high transaction costs. MyClimate only invests in avoidance projects, not sinks. MyClimate currently supports biomass projects in India, solar hot water heaters in Eritrea and Costa Rica and methane projects in South Africa. They are verified against international emission reduction standards and MyClimate's sustainable development criteria.

Pricing: US$30.00 per tCO_2e

Volume: 30,000tCO_2e in 2005; projected 200,000tCO_2e in 2006

Primary Markets: Business and individual travelers, travel agents

* * * * *

*Native*Energy

www.nativeenergy.com

Location: Charlotte, Vermont, USA

Business Model: *Native*Energy sells Green Tags from wind farm projects in the US to individuals and businesses who wish to offset carbon emissions. Unlike most Green Tag providers who sell tags as they are generated by existing generators, *Native*Energy uses Green Tags to help build new wind farms. The company seeks out wind farms under development that need to be sure of long-term Green Tag revenues to complete development and through the *Wind*Builders^{sm} programme it purchases all the Green Tags to be generated by the wind farms over their expected operating life – usually 25 years, providing up-front financial support. Projects include two large-scale wind turbines and a number of other smaller scale wind and methane projects all on Native American land.

Partners and Clients: Clients have included the Dave Matthews Band, Ben & Jerry's and the Timberland Company. *Wind*Builders is Climate Cool certified by the Climate Neutral Network.

Pricing: US$13.50 per tCO_2e

Volume: N/A

Primary Markets: Businesses and individuals

* * * * *

Natsource

www.natsource.com/buycredits/

Location: New York, New York, US

Business Model: Natsource's emissions business is comprised of three integrated business units: (1) asset management services; (2) advisory and research services; and (3) transaction services. Selling offset credits is not one of the organization's primary activities. However, in association with DuPont and Blue Source which are supporting the Ad Council and Environmental Defense campaign to Fight Global Warming, Natsource now offers offsets for individuals at the retail level. Purchase registered carbon dioxide equivalent (CO_2e) offset credits, are from select DuPont and Blue Source carbon-reducing projects.

Partners and Clients: All purchasable offset credits have been serialized by Environmental Resources Trust, Inc. Natsource was selected by Environmental Defense as an approved offset credit seller.

Volume: N/A

Primary Markets: Retail, brokerage

* * * * *

Offsetter's Climate Neutral Society

http://offsetters.com/index.htm

Location: Vancouver BC

Business Model: Offsetters Climate Neutral Society (OCNS) is a Canada based not-for-profit organization, which invests in local and international renewable energy and energy efficiency projects that not only reduce greenhouse gas emissions to the atmosphere, but also enhance ecosystems and provide wider benefits to the people living around them. Their offset projects are collaborative with Climate Care. Projects include efficient lighting programmes in South Africa, biogass digesters in India, reforestation in Uganda, and more efficient cooking stoves in Bangladesh.

Offsetters was established through the Institute for Resources, Environment and Sustainability at the University of British Columbia and the James Martin Institute for Science and Civilization at the University of Oxford. The Offsetters website has a flight emissions calculator and also provides options for individuals to offset their lifestyle greenhouse gas emissions and become climate friendly.

Partners and Clients: With support from the International Airshed Strategy and from the Climate Change Division of Pacific & Yukon Region Offsetters has partnered with Environment Canada in reducing GHG emissions.

Pricing: $16.00 (CAD) per tCO_2e

Volume: 2006 is Offsetters' first year in operation

Primary Markets: Individuals

* * * * *

Prima Klima

www.prima-klima-weltweit.de/english/intro.php3?top=english

Location: Dusseldorf, Germany

Business Model: Prima Klima finances sink projects through funds primarily provided by the industrial and service sector. The company does not follow the Kyoto carbon accounting rules and uses its own 'Catalogue of Criteria' modelled on the Forestry Stewardship Council principles to select participating projects. Products are sold for €75 to offset $1tCO_2$ every year for 50 years.

Projects, Partners and Clients: Prima Klima has reforested and implemented CO_2-related ecological measures through over 80 projects on more than 2,000 hectares of land in Germany and more than 1,200 hectares in 18 other countries around the world. The company has received grants of more than €2.2 million for tree planting and forest regeneration.

Pricing: €1.50 per tCO_2e (net present value figured at $5.65 per tCO_2e, NPV figured at a six per cent discount rate and assuming a constant delivery of tons of carbon credits over time).

Volume: $31,000tCO_2e$ per year

Solar Electric Light Fund

www.self.org/cnc.asp

Location: Washington, D.C., USA

Business Model: Solar Electric Light Fund (SELF) allows individuals to offset carbon emissions by financing renewable energy to off-grid rural areas in the developing world. By replacing the use of kerosene and diesel, each system prevents 6 tons of CO_2 from entering the atmosphere over its 20-year life.

Certified Product: Carbon Neutral Club

Projects, Partners and Clients: On average, SELF installs 1,000 solar PV systems a year in developing nation villages.

Pricing: \$10.00 per tCO_2e

Volume: 6000tCO_2e per year

Primary Markets: Businesses and individuals

* * * * *

Sustainable Travel International

www.sustainabletravelinternational.org

Location: Boulder, Colorado

Business Model: Sustainable Travel International offers offsets to individuals and institutions through a partnership with MyClimate. Sustainable Travel International uses an online calculator to help clients calculate the GHG offsets associated with their air and ground travel. According to the Sustainable Travel website, 'it costs approximately \$9 US per 500 miles traveled and \$18 US per 1000 miles travelled. Our carbon calculator also takes into consideration greenhouse gasses other than CO_2 and uses a RFI factor of 2. In addition, we compute the average cost to compensate for of a ton of CO_2 in a climatic protection project. These two factors – the emissions and the costs of the emission reduction – result in our final pricing.'

Partners and Clients: MyClimate's offsets are verified according to The Gold Standard.

Pricing: US\$17.50 per tCO_2e

Volume: See MyClimate numbers

Primary Markets: Individuals and businesses

TerraPass

www.terrapass.com

Location: Menlo Park, California, USA

Business Model: TerraPass offers motorists a way to offset their car emissions through the purchase of emissions offsets. It does not support a specific project portfolio but works with wholesalers and through the CCX to purchase credits from renewable energy projects and greenhouse gas abatement projects (primarily methane capture and avoidance). Uniquely, it publishes its transaction history online. In 2006 the company expects to continue investment in current projects rather than source new transactions, moving to a project portfolio model. The company strives to divide its portfolio equally, but in 2005 50 per cent of the funds went to methane capture projects, 30 per cent to clean energy and 20 per cent to energy efficiency.

Partners and Clients: Terrapass is third-party certified by Green-e. Ford customers can offset their vehicles' with Terrapass through Ford's Greener Miles programme.

Pricing: US$8.00–11.00 per tCO_2e

Volume: $10,000tCO_2e$

Primary Markets: Individuals

* * * * *

Trees for the Future

www.treesftf.org/main.htm

Location: Silver Spring, Maryland, USA

Business Model: Through its Global Cooling Center, Trees for the Future sells carbon certificates to offset travel and business operations and plants trees in the developing world. It plants approximately 400 trees for a $40 product, and it estimates that each tree absorbs $1tCO_2$ over its lifespan. There is no third-party verification. Trees for the Future supports small-scale projects around the world and is soliciting new projects on an ongoing basis. It is primarily focused on the sustainable development and agroforestry aspects of projects, in addition to their ability to generate carbon credits.

Pricing: $0.10 per tCO_2e (net present value figured at $0.43, NPV figured at a 6 per cent discount rate and assuming constant delivery of tons of carbon credits over time).

Volume: N/A – 3.1 million trees planted in 2005

Primary Markets: Individuals

Appendix 5

Examples of Institutional Buyers

Table A5.1

Company	*Buy from*	*Why buy*	*What type*	*Price*	*Volume* tCO_2e
AGL	Project developers	Product	Renewable energy/methane	Unknown	Unknown
Alcoa	Internal projects and REC providers	Carbon targets	Renewable energy/forestry	Unknown	250,000 (by 2020)
Avis Europe	Retailer (Carbon Neutral Company)	Carbon targets	Mix	Unknown	Unknown
BP Global Choice	Project developers	Product	Energy	Unknown	500,000
Cinergy	Project developers	Carbon targets	Forestry/mix	Unknown	Potentially millions
Cooperative Bank	Retailer (Climate Care)	Offset 1/5 of emissions from mortgage loans	Mix	£225,000	43,000
Entergy	Project portfolio	Carbon targets	Mix	$5.3 million	3.5 million since 2001
FIFA World Cup	Project portfolio	Carbon neutral	Mix	€1.3 million	100,000
HSBC	Projects – tender	Carbon neutral	Technology/ energy	$750,000	150,000
Interface	Projects and Retailer (Climate Care)	Product and internal emissions	Mix	Varies	250,000 +
MECU	Retailer (Greenfleet)	Product	Forestry	Unknown	8,000
Origin Energy	Projects	Product	Mix	Unknown	Unknown
Radio Taxis	Retailer (CarbonNeutral)	Carbon neutral	Mix	£99,840	24,000
Swiss Re	Retailer (World Bank Development Carbon Fund)	Carbon neutral	CDM	Unknown	37,000
Western Power	Projects	Product	Mix	Unknown	Unknown

Europe

Avis Europe

www.avis-europe.com/content-22

Avis Europe has developed and committed to a greenhouse plan to reduce and offset carbon emissions from its corporate operations and to encourage customers to offset emissions from rentals. Its data collection and analysis is conducted by the Edinburgh Centre for Carbon Management and works exclusively with The CarbonNeutral Company to purchase offsets.

* * * * *

Cooperative Bank

www.co-operativebank.co.uk

The Cooperative Bank pays to offset 1/5 of the carbon emissions generated from mortgage customers' homes every year the mortgage exists. Working through Climate Care, the bank donated £225,000 to offset 43,000tCO_2e in 2004.

* * * * *

FIFA World Cup

http://greengoal.fifaworldcup.yahoo.net

The 2006 FIFA World Cup in Germany initiated a 'Green Goal' of meeting measurable environment protection targets, including ensuring the event is carbon neutral. The event's climate impact was reduced by increased energy efficiency, use of renewable energy sources and support for environment-friendly transportation. After such efforts it was estimated 100,000 tons of greenhouse gases would be emitted, mainly by vehicle traffic, due to the event. To offset these emissions a total of €1.3 million was invested in climate protection projects in developing countries. For example, 1/3 of the needed credits will be generated by investments in biogas production facilities in Tamil Nadu, a region of South-east India. The biogas facilities financed by Green Goal convert cow dung into gas, and are estimated to save some 30,000 tons of emissions by creating a substitute for wood and kerosene when cooking. The price paid to support this project is around €10/ton.

* * * * *

HSBC

www.hsbc.com/hsbc/csr/environment/the-challenge-of-climate-change;brochid=DMIWBNSK50XUZQFIYN0SGWQ

HSBC announced its intentions to become carbon neutral by 2006 and met its target by October 2005. As the first major bank to go carbon neutral, HSBC accomplished its goal initially through on-site energy efficiency and the purchase of renewable energy and then undertook a pilot offset project to neutralize its remaining 170,000tCO_2. With the help of The Climate Group and ICF Consulting, the bank initiated a tendering process that attracted over 100 project submissions. HSBC ultimately spent $750,000 for projects in New Zealand, Australia, Germany and India at an average cost of $4.43 per t$CO_2$.

Selected projects were chosen by an HSBC task force based on their vintages (2005 and 2006), size (projects had to offset at least 10,000tCO_2), technology (given priority over sinks) and country (Brazil, Mexico, India and China were original priorities). The majority of offsets were provided by Meridian Energy from its wind farm in New Zealand, for which HSBC paid approximately $560,000 for 125,000t$CO_2$. HSBC is now auditing its emissions and offsets through a third party.

* * * * *

Radio Taxis Group

www.radiotaxis.co.uk/master.htm?about-csr

Radio Taxis Group operates as a CarbonNeutral™ company, working with the CarbonNeutral Company to purchase offsets for its fleet of 3000 cabs. As the world's first major carbon neutral taxi company, it is offsetting both its corporate emissions and emissions from transporting its 3.8 million annual customers. Approximately 24,000tCO_2 will be offset per year for £4.16 per tCO_2 through energy (80 per cent) and sink (20 per cent) projects managed by CarbonNeutral. The project began from an initial emission audit conducted by the Edinburgh Centre for Carbon Management, which then suggested strategies for offsetting climate impacts. The deal came at the same time as London announced low-emission standards for cabs. Radio Taxis represents 15 per cent of the London market.

* * * * *

Swiss Re

www.swissre.com

Swiss Re has initiated a ten-year programme to become carbon neutral. This will be accomplished by reducing internal emissions by 15 per cent and investing in the World Bank Community Development Carbon Fund to offset the remaining 85 per cent. The Development Carbon Fund invests in CDM projects. This voluntary initiative makes Swiss Re the largest global financial services company to become greenhouse neutral, reducing the global carbon load by 37,000tCO_2 annually.

North America

Alcoa

www.alcoa.com/global/en/home.asp

Alcoa is a US-based aluminum manufacturer that is aiming to reduce emissions by 25 per cent by 2010 from 1990 levels. This is being achieved through a number of reduction and offset efforts, including the purchase of RECs, on-site energy efficiency, renewable energy and planting trees. Alcoa's Ten Million Trees Program aims to plant 10 million trees by 2020 to absorb 250,000tCO_2. Employees, contractors and suppliers purchase trees from a local supplier and plant them on Alcoa property, private property or in parks, partnering with organizations who can advise on species and locations, such as Greening Australia or TreeLink (Canada).

* * * * *

Cinergy

www.cinergy.com/pdfs/AIRS_12012004_final.pdf

Cinergy is an energy and utility provider operating in the Midwest US of Ohio, Indiana and Kentucky. In 2004 the company voluntarily committed to reducing greenhouse gas emissions to 5 per cent below 2000 levels by 2012. Funds amounting to $21 million have been set aside for on-system (internal) and off-system projects to achieve this goal.

When the programme began in 2004, on-system projects received first priority and provided most of the emissions reductions through energy efficiency improvements and switching the fleet to hybrid cars. Off-system projects focused primarily on forestry. Cinergy solicited forestry projects to offset about 1000tCO_2, working with organizations such as Ducks Unlimited, the Nature Conservancy and Edison Electric Institute to plant trees or in some cases purchase land for reforestation. With these initial efforts, Cinergy estimates costs at $1.66 per t$CO_2$, but this moved toward $5–10t$CO_2$ in 2005 as new, more expensive on- and off-site projects were added to the portfolio.

To date Cinergy has not purchased credits through the market but may do so in the future in order to meet its goal. Depending on energy demand and corresponding generation requirements (which in turn depend on a number of factors including weather patterns and economic growth), the company estimates having to reduce emissions by 2–6 million tCO_2 per year. While 1–2 million tons are expected to be reduced through on-system reductions, several million tons may be provided via off-system credits. Cinergy is currently evaluating its options and conducting risk analysis around purchasing European versus American offsets – the former being more expensive but verified and the latter operating in an unregulated market that provides little assurance.

Entergy

www.entergy.com/content/our_community/pdfs/ghg.pdf

Entergy is an energy and utilities provider operating in the Southeast US. In 2001 it launched a programme to stabilize carbon emissions from its power plants by setting an 'emission budget' – the target was not to exceed five times 2000 levels in the five years from 2001–2005. This has been achieved so far through $14.8 million of funding for 61 internal emissions-reduction projects and $5.3 million of funding for 13 external projects. External projects have offset 3.5 million tCO_2 since 2001 and included forestry sequestration through the Tensas River National Wildlife Refuge (with the US Fish & Wildlife Service), geo-sequestration from Blue Source Inc., sustainable forestry to which Entergy owns the carbon credits, the purchase of RECs from methane capture at coal mines in Ohio and West Virginia and domestic and international emissions trading.

* * * * *

Interface Carpet

www.interfaceinc.com

Interface Carpet's Cool Carpet programme uses life cycle analysis to determine carbon emissions from carpet production, which it then offsets through its own portfolio of renewable energy, energy efficiency and sink projects, as well as a relationship with Climate Care (see above). The programme is certified through the Climate Neutral Network's Climate Cool™ certification scheme (see above). Projects include an innovative transaction with supplier Invista who generates offset credits through the reduction of nitrous oxide emissions, which are verified by the Cleaner and Greener programme (see above). Other projects include geosequestration from Blue Source and a wind farm in New Zealand through Meridian Energy (and brokered by CO2e.com). Through Climate Care, Interface's offsets contribute to energy reduction projects in South Africa and restoring rainforests in Uganda. Interface also has a company-wide target of reducing US GHG emissions by 15 per cent per unit of production from 2001 to 2010.

Australia

AGL

www.agl.com.au/AGLNew/Your+home/AGL+Green+Choice/AGL+Green+Balance.htm

AGL offers residential customers the option of purchasing renewable energy through its Green Energy programme or offsetting emissions through Green Balance. Green Power is sourced from Australian Greenhouse Office accredited green power wind, solar, biogas and landfill (methane) projects through a combination of AGL owned and operated and partner sites. Green Balance provides offsets through Greenhouse Friendly accredited projects, primarily the reduction of methane at landfill sites.

* * * * *

BP Global Choice

www.bp.com.au/globalchoice/default.asp

BP Global Choice™ is an Australia-based non-profit programme that invests funds into projects to reduce emissions, equivalent to those generated by motorists. Member companies pay a small premium on top of the fuel they purchase for their fleet, choosing a percentage of emissions they wish to offset. Or companies can buy BP Ultimate or BP Autogas, and BP automatically offsets 100 per cent of emissions. Cost to businesses range from $35–$70 per vehicle annually. To date, the programme has offset 1.25 million tCO_2. In 2004, BP purchased 600,000tCO_2 offset credits; in 2005, it purchased 500,000tCO_2.

Initially working with the Commonwealth Bank of Australia, BP identified Australia-based offset projects, including fuel switching in a meat rendering plant, capturing landfill gas, renewable energy and cleaner technology. Projects are independently verified by the Australian Greenhouse Office, which provides Greenhouse Friendly accreditation, and are assessed for their additionality (over regulatory requirements and business as usual). One project, the Denison Trough Joint Venture, is run in conjunction with Origin Energy, who manage the project offsets and sell credits exclusively to BP for the Global Choice programme. BP purchases credits directly from project developers and does not go through a retailer or wholesaler. While current contracts supply enough abatement credits, BP will consider other projects to add to its portfolio.

BP is currently considering the viability of expanding the Global Choice to other countries.

* * * * *

MECU

www.mecu.com.au/index_general.asp?menuid=020.090.010&size=normal

MECU is a financial services organization that is redesigning mainstream banking products to include economic, social and environmental features, such as its goGreen® Car Loan product. Through goGreen, MECU offsets all of the greenhouse gas emissions produced by the car for the life of the loan. This is accomplished in partnership with Greenfleet (see above), and as of June 2005, MECU had planted over 31,000 trees, which will absorb about 8000tCO_2 annually. MECU works exclusively with Greenfleet and is not pursuing other carbon offset schemes at this time.

Origin Energy

www.originenergy.com.au

Origin Energy invests in a number of projects and offers customers several products aimed at reducing greenhouse emissions. The GreenEarth Electricity product offering allows residential customers to purchase renewable energy accredited by the Australian Greenhouse Office's Green Power programme. GreenEarth Gas includes the purchase of emissions offsets and is accredited by the Australian Government's Greenhouse Friendly programme. Offset credits are provided by the burning of methane or capturing greenhouse gas emissions from landfill sites. In addition, Origin is involved in the Denison Trough Joint Venture, which has offset 700,000tCO_2 since 2001 by eliminating waste gas in a gas production field. As the owner of the project's emission reduction units, Origin sells credits to BP Australia, which it uses in its BP Global Choice product offering.

* * * * *

Western Power

www.westernpower.com.au/home/index.html

Western Power offers residential customers the option of purchasing renewable energy through its NaturalPower offering or offsetting emissions through Earth Friendly power. NaturalPower is created by Green Power accredited wind, hydro, biomass and solar generators. Earth Friendly is accredited as Greenhouse Friendly and includes projects such as extracting and burning methane from landfill, landfill diversion (reduced waste), fuel substitution and forest sequestration.

Examples of brokers/wholesalers

Evolution Markets Ltd

www.evomarkets.com

Location: White Plains, NY, USA

Business Model: Evolution Markets specializes in structuring transactions and providing consulting and risk-management advisory services for environmental credit markets, energy markets and other emerging markets (such as weather derivatives). As a carbon offset provider, Evolution Markets brokers CERs, ERUs and VERs. The company also provides carbon market advisory services and carbon finance services to project managers.

Primary Markets: Institutional buyers and sellers

EcoSecurities

www.ecosecurities.com

Location: Dublin, Ireland

Business Model: EcoSecurities' primary focus is on creating and selling CERs and ERUs for the regulated carbon market. However, the firm also sells VERs to corporations wishing to voluntarily offset emissions. EcoSecurities manages a diverse set of large portfolios of greenhouse gas emission reduction projects distributed over more than 25 countries and using more than 20 technologies. Hence, buyers can choose from a wide variety of technologies, greenhouse gas reduction methodologies, geographic areas, risk profiles, terms, volumes and sustainability co-benefits.

Primary Markets: Institutional buyers and sellers

* * * * *

CO2e.com

www.CO2e.com

Location: London, UK

Business model: CO2e.com Ltd (CO2e) is an environmental finance and brokerage firm, owned by Cantor Fitzgerald and Mitsui. CO2e works in the international carbon markets – both compliance and voluntary – has a European desk brokering screen-based and voice-brokered transactions of EUAs, arranges long-term power purchase agreements for renewable energy and helps provide structured finance solutions to projects in these market places. CO2e has brokered tens of millions of tons of emission reductions, from large, small, industrial, renewable energy, energy efficiency and forestry projects from across the globe. Locations of projects include South America, Asia, Oceania, Africa, the Caribbean and North America.

Primary Markets: Institutional buyers and sellers

* * * * *

Natsource

(See Appendix 4)

Index